Jimmy Doolittle

JIMMY DOOLITTLE

Master of the Calculated Risk

CARROLL V. GLINES

VNR VAN NOSTRAND REINHOLD COMPANY
NEW YORK CINCINNATI TORONTO LONDON MELBOURNE

To

DOOLITTLE'S TOKYO RAIDERS

First published in paperback in 1980
Copyright © 1972, 1980 by Carroll V. Glines
Library of Congress Catalog Card Number 79-56938
ISBN 0-442-23102-4

Van Nostrand Reinhold Company
A Division of Litton Educational Publishing, Inc.
135 West 50th Street, New York, NY 10020

Van Nostrand Reinhold Ltd.
1410 Birchmount Road, Scarborough, Ontario M1P 2E7

Van Nostrand Reinhold Australia Pty. Ltd.
17 Queen Street, Mitcham, Victoria 3132

Van Nostrand Reinhold Company Ltd.
Molly Millars Lane, Wokingham, Berkshire, England RG11 2PY

Cloth edition published 1972 by Macmillan Publishing Co., Inc.
Second cloth impression 1974

16 15 14 13 12 11 10 9 8 7 6 5 4 3 2 1

Contents

1. "Nome Town Boy
Makes Good!"

THE BOW OF THE U.S.S. *Hornet*, the navy's newest carrier, see-sawed up and down through the waves as it plowed westward toward Japan. As the bow dipped downward, it smashed into the green water, sending shudders throughout the ship. As the bow rose upward, rivers of water came running down the broad deck and under the sixteen twin-engine Army Air Force's B-25 bombers lashed firmly to the deck. Sailors slipped and slid as they went about their duties throughout the ship.

Escorting the *Hornet* nearby were other ships, including the carrier *Enterprise*. It was their job to see that the *Hornet* got within about 450 miles of the Japanese coast. It was the *Hornet*'s job to launch the twin-engine bombers for a raid against Japan. The date: April 18, 1942.

The United States had been at war for over four months by this time and the morale of its people had never been lower. After the surprise attack on Pearl Harbor on December 7, 1941, Japanese military forces had taken Wake Island and Guam, the British garrisons at Hong Kong and Singapore, and had gained control of all of southeast Asia. In addition, almost all of the Philippines had been conquered, except for the troops defending the small island of Corregidor.

As the Japanese forces had moved swiftly in the Pacific, Germany and Italy had promptly declared war on the United States. For the first time in its history, the United States found itself embarked upon an all-out two-front global war. If ever a victory was needed, it was at this time in American history.

While the navy task force continued its westward journey, army crews slept fitfully below decks. They had been thoroughly briefed by their leader, a short, balding man with a quick smile, an athletic bounce to his walk, and a daredevil reputation based upon his years as a racing and test pilot. Although he had received a degree as Doctor of Aeronautical Sciences from Massachusetts Institute of Technology and was a top-notch scientist, his public image was that of a devil-may-care stunt pilot whose only interest in life seemed to be flying fast planes, winning air race trophies, and setting speed records. What the public did not seem to realize was that this man's reasons for wanting to push the speed barriers back was to improve man's knowledge about airplanes. Besides winning racing trophies, he had been the first to span the United States by air in less than a day, first to fly an outside loop, and first to take off, fly, and land on instruments to make "blind" flying a reality. He had also pioneered in the manufacture of high-octane aviation gasoline, which made bigger and more powerful engines possible.

"Name's Doolittle," he had said, matter-of-factly, two months before when he asked for volunteers for "a dangerous mission against the enemy." That name, to the young pilots and crews of the four B-25 squadrons from which they had come, meant adventure. If the great Jimmy Doolittle was going to lead a combat mission, they wanted to be part of it.

Although they had helped modify the planes and practiced taking off in short distances, these men did not know they were going to be expected to take land bombers off a carrier until they had set out to sea and Jimmy Doolittle had briefed them on their mission. They were to bomb military targets in Tokyo, Japan's capital, and four other large cities, and then fly on to bases in China. The navy would get them as close as possible before launching. If the carriers were undetected, Doolittle himself would take off at dusk and bomb Tokyo with fire bombs. The fires would serve as a beacon for the other fifteen crews. After the bombs were dropped, all planes were to head for landing fields in China for daylight landings. The plan was simple. All the crews had to do now was wait until the navy got them to a point about 450 miles east of Tokyo.

One by one, crew members awakened in their bunks below decks and started to prepare for breakfast. Suddenly, the chilling klaxon horn blasted through the carrier, followed by the order, "Army pilots, man your planes! Army pilots, man your planes!"

The eighty men who were to fly those sixteen bombers knew what had happened. The task force had been discovered by a Japanese radio-equipped fishing boat that had flashed a warning message to Tokyo. While destroyers fired at the boat and sank it, the B-25 crews jammed their belongings into their flight bags and raced to their planes. Spare crew members who were aboard the carrier but who would not go on the mission pulled off engine covers and untied ropes. Navy deck handlers helped position the planes for takeoff.

When his crew was all aboard, Doolittle started the engines of his B-25 and warmed them up. When he was satisfied that the plane was ready to go, he taxied into position where two lines had been painted along the deck. If he kept his left main wheel and nose wheel on those lines during the takeoff run, his right wing would clear the carrier's "island" on the right. It wouldn't be easy. The carrier was steaming ahead at full speed through very rough seas. One moment the deck was pointing skyward and the next it seemed to be plunging beneath the green waves.

On the deck of the carrier a launch officer gave the signal for Doolittle to rev up his engines to full speed. At the proper moment after the bow had smashed into a wave and the deck began to tilt upward, the signal was given for Doolittle to release his brakes.

The heavily-laden bomber slowly inched forward, gathered speed, and was airborne. Cheers went up from the navy crewmen. The great Jimmy Doolittle had another aviation "first" to his credit—first to take a land-based bomber off a carrier for a combat mission.

One by one, the young pilots in the other fifteen bombers edged their planes into position and took off. Because they had to take off early, each plane would barely have enough gas to get to China after bombing their targets. Instead of flying formation, each plane was to make its own way to the assigned target and ultimate destination. Since visibility was bad, few of the eighty men saw any of the other planes after takeoff.

As the planes sped westward, the radio message sent by the enemy fishing boat had been received in Japan, but it could not be verified. Consequently, only a few Japanese naval officers knew of the possibility of a raid by American planes and no one thought they would be land-based bombers equipped to fly 2,000 miles. If a raid was imminent, it was thought that the Americans would have to bring their carriers in close to shore, use short-range carrier planes, and then try to escape out to sea afterward.

The surprise that Doolittle had hoped for became a reality. Shortly after noon, when thousands of Japanese were eating their midday meal, Doolittle's bombardier, Sergeant Fred Braemer, opened the bomb bay and dropped the bombs on a factory near the center of downtown Tokyo. As soon as the last bomb was gone, Doolittle jammed the nose of the B-25 downward and skimmed the rooftops as he headed southward on the escape route.

Although there was no air raid alert, enemy planes were in the air on routine patrol and training exercises as the fifteen planes following Doolittle raced toward Tokyo and the other cities. Smoke from the fires set by Doolittle's bombs curled upward and the Tokyo air raid system came to life. Some of the American planes were intercepted and one B-25 pilot, finding that his guns were not operating, dropped his bombs in Tokyo Bay. The others fought off the attackers successfully. Only one plane was hit by enemy machine-gun fire but it was only slightly damaged.

The attacking B-25s headed southward and then westward across the China Sea after all bombs were released. Miraculously, every plane had escaped. Now the task was to find three landing fields located in a mountainous area of China. It wasn't going to be easy. Since they had left the carrier far ahead of schedule, the planes would now arrive over China in darkness— if their gas held out.

After takeoff, one plane's crew had quickly found that both engines were consuming far too much fuel. After dropping their bombs, the pilot decided to set his course for Vladivostok, a Russian city north of Korea, where he landed safely. To the crew's surprise, they were promptly interned and held prisoners for the next thirteen months.

The other fifteen planes had a different kind of luck. As they neared the Chinese mainland, the weather slowly deteriorated. They encountered low ceilings and rain. The darkness added to their difficulties. To make matters worse, the radio homing beacons that were to guide them to their airfields were not operating because the Chinese thought the oncoming planes were Japanese, since they were not on schedule.

When the ceiling and visibility got dangerously low, some pilots, including Doolittle, climbed to higher altitudes. If their gas ran out before they sighted any fields, they were going to order their crews to bail out. One by one, the men in eleven planes did strap on their parachutes and jump into the rainy blackness.

The pilots of the other four aircraft elected to crash-land their planes either in the water offshore or along a beach. By about 9:30 P.M. on the evening of April 18, 1942, all sixteen planes were out of the air. Unfortunately, only one of them would ever fly again.

It took many days for Doolittle to round up his crews or find out what had happened to them. One man had died bailing out. Two more had drowned after their plane was ditched. Four men of one crew were badly injured; one of them so badly that his leg had to be amputated. Eight men had been captured by the Japanese, branded "war criminals" and destined to be tortured. Of these, three men were to be executed and one would die of malnutrition. The remaining four men would suffer forty months of

solitary confinement before being rescued by American para-
troopers at war's end.

As the news slowly filtered in to Doolittle, who had made his
way to Chungking, he became very depressed. The raid he had
led was his first combat mission, although he had learned to fly
during World War I. He thought it would be his last. Although
all sixteen planes had survived the run over Japan, all of them
were now lost to the American cause. As far as he was concerned, he had failed as a combat leader. He felt sure that he
would be court-martialed when he returned to the United States.

The news of the raid against Japan hit the Allied world suddenly and at a moment when morale of the people in the countries fighting Japan, Italy, and Germany was at its lowest point.
The effect was immediate. Newspaper headlines screamed:
TOKYO BOMBED! and radios blared that American bombers
had paid the Japanese back for the "unprovoked and dastardly
attack" they had made at Pearl Harbor.

While the fact that some Japanese cities had beem bombed
was not a secret, the fact that the attacking planes had taken off
from a U.S. carrier was not released and remained an official
secret for a year.

For several days, the public did not know who had led the raid
but within hours of its completion, Doolittle was promoted from
Lieutenant Colonel to Brigadier General, skipping the rank of
Colonel. When he found out the fate of his men, he was ordered
to return to the States, where it was acknowledged that the
famous flier with the famous grin had indeed led the raid that
gave new hope to the Allies and provided a boost in morale when
it was most needed. Instead of a court-martial, Jimmy Doolittle,
the man who thought he had failed miserably as a combat
leader, was ordered to the White House. There, President Franklin Delano Roosevelt hung a star-sprinkled blue ribbon around
his neck. Attached to it was the Congressional Medal of Honor,
highest award for bravery that a grateful nation can bestow on a
military man.

"Thank you, Mr. President," Doolittle said. He accepted the

award from his commander in chief but did not think he had earned it. Even today, he does not believe he should have been so honored. "I'll spend the rest of my life trying to earn it," he says.

When it was officially confirmed that Jimmy Doolittle had led the Tokyo raid, the editor of the *Nome Nugget*, the only newspaper in the remote village of Nome, Alaska, went back into his print shop and set the day's headline in the largest type he had:

NOME TOWN BOY MAKES GOOD!

He had good reason to make his readers remember Jimmy Doolittle. The same man who had become so famous as a racing pilot and now as a combat hero had indeed grown up in Nome and had sold the *Nugget* to earn his first pocket money. It was in Nome, fabled destination of fortune seekers of an earlier day, that the Daredevil Scientist got his start.

2. A Fighter Is Born

THE WORD "GOLD" HAS captured the minds and souls of men for centuries. Whenever it has been discovered, men have given up families and friends and risked their lives as they succumbed to the lure of easy fortune.

The California Gold Rush of 1849 had been inspired by the discovery of the valuable yellow mineral at Sutter's Mill. Thousands of men, women, and children stampeded to the west coast of the continent to gamble their futures on finding their share of it. The promise was short-lived, however, and only a few men ever improved their position in life by actually sinking a pick into a gold vein or panning the telltale sparkle from the gravel of a mountain stream.

But the get-rich-quick lure that has tempted men for so long does not die completely, it seems. There were other gold rushes in American history and the Gold Rush of '98 to the Klondike area of Northwest Canada has become a part of American legend. Although gold had first been discovered along the Yukon River as early as 1872, it was not until 1896 that a new stampede to the north began. On August 17, of that year, George W. Carmack's Indian wife, Kate, discovered gold while washing out a frying pan in Bonanza Creek, one of the streams leading into the Klondike River. When the S. S. *Portland* docked in Seattle eleven months later with the gold dust purchased from those who had cashed in on Carmack's discovery, the newspapers of the world announced that a "ton of gold" had arrived from the fabulous Klondike.

Many people started north in the fall of 1897 and about 2,000 arrived before the rivers froze and thus prohibited boat travel. The real stampede of humans began in 1898 when an estimated 200,000 people started for the Klondike. With so many people searching for the elusive metal, it was inevitable that many would follow the Klondike to the Yukon River and down the Yukon into Alaska, where occasional finds were made but nothing compared to the $50 million in gold taken from the Klondike.

Although the "Trail of Ninety-Eight" quickly cooled, there was one more discovery a year later that sent another wave of adventurers northward. This was a report that gold had been discovered on the beach at Nome, a small village on the southern shores of Alaska's Seward Peninsula. The report was true and represented the greatest "poor-man's diggings" ever found. All a man needed was a shovel, a bucket, a "rocker" box, and a wheelbarrow. Two months after old, ailing John Hummel had stumbled on the new find, 2,000 people were at work on the beaches and more than $1,000,000 in gold was extracted from the sand.

As was to be expected, when the steamers carrying the Nome gold dust arrived at West Coast ports, there was a new surge of interest in going north in search of quick fortunes. Professional promoters took advantage of the situation to form transportation and mining companies. During the summer of 1900, more than 15,000 people had reached Nome. Among them was Frank H. Doolittle, a carpenter who had gone to the Klondike in 1897 and had followed each new rumor of gold down the Yukon until he had reached Nome. His wife, Rosa, and his six-month-old son, James Harold, born December 14, 1896, had been left behind in Alameda, California.

The scene that greeted Rosa and now three-year-old Jim at

Nome in 1900 was unbelievably chaotic. Thousands of tons of freight were piled high along the beach. As one historian noted:

> Everything was in an appalling state of confusion: machinery, all sorts of supplies, hay, grain, lumber, hardware, provisions, liquor, tents, stoves, sewing machines, mirrors, bar fixtures—everything that one may imagine. The delivery of goods to their rightful owners was next to impossible. The steamship companies claimed that their responsibilities for the goods ceased when the goods went over the ship's side.*

During the summer of 1900 there was a solid row of tents stretching five miles along the Nome beach. The main street—the only thoroughfare—was a surging mass of humanity at all hours because it never got dark. A few buildings had been completed and men worked furiously trying to build more before the inevitable early freeze of late August.

Thousands of people slept out-of-doors in tents and in lean-to shacks. Lumber was scarce and all of it had to be brought in by ship or cut from driftwood logs that occasionally washed ashore. The only fuel was scrap lumber or coal, also hauled from "The South 48."

As the population increased, so did crime. Unfortunately, Alaska was a land without effective government or police at this time. As a result, citizens had to take the law into their own hands. Disputes were settled by guns, knives, or fists. Despite the almost impossible conditions, Nome survived. Houses were built, streets were laid out, and a semblance of law and order prevailed.

The need for a man who was handy with his hands was great and Frank Doolittle, an experienced carpenter, prospered. On one of the last ships leaving Nome in 1899, he had sent a letter to Rosa and asked her to bring their son Jimmy with her to Nome the following spring. Although she was unprepared for the mixture of Eskimos, miners, gamblers, trappers, and promoters, she

* Hulley, Clarence C., *Alaska: Past and Present*, p. 266. Portland, Oregon: Binsfords and Mort, 1958.

Jimmy Doolittle grew up in Nome, Alaska, where his father was a carpenter. This photo was taken in 1902 just before he started first grade. (*Photo courtesy of the Robert C. Reeve Collection*)

bravely dug into her chores to make the house her husband had built into a home for the three of them.

The days passed into months and Frank Doolittle prospered as a carpenter. He built houses for those who could afford them. In his spare time, he built a house for his own family. Sitting on pilings driven into the permafrost, the unpainted wooden building would be called a shack by today's standards. But it was home to the Doolittles—even if it did have to be straightened up each spring when the ground thawed out.

Living in Nome in those days was a battle for survival—not just survival against the bitter Arctic climate but against hunger and want. For a boy, and an undersized one at that, life was also a constant battle for survival against bigger boys who delighted in pushing smaller ones around.

It was in this environment that Jimmy Doolittle, small for his age and with long, curly hair, went out to play. It wasn't long before he had his first battle. He described it later:

> I was walking along the beach alone one day looking for things that might have washed ashore when an Eskimo boy came along. For some reason I cannot recall now, he started pushing me around. Being inexperienced, I was fearless and lit into him with all the fury that a young lad of about five years old can muster. After a few minutes of furious wrestling and flailing, I managed to poke the fellow in the nose. Blood gushed down his face and onto his clothes. We both stopped fighting and were both suddenly frightened. It was the first time either of us had seen human blood. He thought he was dying. I thought I had killed an Eskimo. We both ran home to our mothers.

Although there were no known witnesses to this episode on the beach, the word spread about the Doolittle kid. Whenever he went out to play, somebody would deliberately pick a fight with him—to their inevitable dismay—because Jimmy Doolittle had found out that it was easy to draw blood and thus win a fight by doubling up his fists and aiming for an opponent's nose.

By the time the curly-haired Doolittle entered first grade in school, he had earned a measure of respect among some of his contemporaries. But the first day of school started a new round of fights. He was kidded so much about his girl-like long curls that he rushed home and demanded that his mother cut them off. She did, but the scrappy Jimmy found that his schoolmates still liked to see him fight. Each new kid in the Nome grammar school had to try to whip the small Doolittle boy in order to be accepted in the gang. As a result, Doolittle would find himself accosted by bigger boys who would promptly start to push him around, egged on by a gang of Jimmy's schoolmates. With many fights to his credit during the pre-teen-age years, he learned to take care of himself.

Wiry, tough and highly competitive in spirit, Jimmy sought to excel in everything he tackled. He told the author:

> There were two kinds of heroes to the kids of Nome in those days— dog team drivers and runners. I didn't have any dogs, so I ran.
> We had a large gym and the men would run 100- and 200-mile races—believe it or not—and almost every kid in town ran. I ran one time until I collapsed. Years later, I was told that I had a heart murmur, which gave me a little trouble on flying physical exams. They tell me it was probably caused by over-exertion when very small.

In the summer of 1904, Jimmy and his father made a quick trip to Seattle by ship. Now an impressionable seven years old, the few days in a large city were memorable. He had no memories of his days before going to Nome so that the sights of a busy metropolitan area were a new experience. He saw his first automobile, train, and trolley car. He saw modern stores and houses with paint on them. "My values changed right then and there," he said. "I saw everything in a new perspective and I wanted very much to be a part of the exciting life I saw so briefly on that memorable trip."

Jimmy returned to Nome, "but everything seemed suddenly smaller." He got a job selling the *Nome Nugget*, the town's famous tabloid newspaper, and the Seattle papers when they came in. He began to read not only the papers but every book he could find. He soon built up an almost overwhelming desire to see the world "outside." Jimmy resolved that when he was old enough, he was going to leave the fabled beaches of Nome and seek his fortune elsewhere.

The restlessness of the boy may have been shared by his mother. In 1908, Mrs. Doolittle and Jimmy left Nome. Mr. Doolittle, a carpenter by trade but an adventurer by inclination, stayed in Alaska and followed every gold rush or rumor of one until he died in 1917. Meanwhile, Jimmy and his mother began a new life in Los Angeles, California, where the boy would become a man and the man would become both respected and honored for his contributions to aeronautics—a word that was just beginning to apply to "aeroplanes"—or those motorized gliders that the Wright brothers had invented.

3. A Lesson in Sportsmanship

ALTHOUGH JIMMY DOOLITTLE WOULD one day win a Doctor of Aeronautical Science degree, he was not considered a brilliant student in his years at the Los Angeles Manual Arts High School. Like many boys in their early teens, he preferred to do things with his hands—either clenched for boxing or working on lathes and gasoline engines.

In the clenched fist department, it didn't take long for the scrappy Doolittle kid to become known for his wild swinging punch and his ability to lick taller and heavier fellows. One day after a schoolyard scrap a teacher of English named Forest Bailey took Jimmy aside. "Look, young fellow," he said, "I know a little about boxing and you're going to get hurt badly one of these days. You get mad when you fight. If you lose your temper, you're going to lose a fight because you let your emotions instead of your head rule your body. Think about that. If you really want to learn how to box, I'll teach you."

Mr. Bailey did teach Jimmy that he could learn to fight without being angry. He convinced the short-armed Doolittle that his flailing style was wasteful because the shortest distance to an opponent's body was a straight line and a punch that travels the shortest distance arrives with more power. He also taught his eager pupil how to bob and weave around an opponent's attack and to keep his right hand ready to strike the moment the other fellow's guard was down.

Jimmy learned that boxing with gloves on and under established rules was both art and science because it required a certain amount of talent plus an ability to analyze an opponent's style and strategy and to devise first a defense and then an offense in order to win.

And win Jimmy did. He quickly proved himself the master of his 105-pound weight class in high school, and Forest Bailey prepared him to enter the Pacific Coast amateur championships at the Los Angeles Athletic Club. Under Bailey's careful tutelage, Jimmy became amateur bantam-weight champion of the West Coast in 1912 at the age of fifteen.

Jimmy's mother did not like her son to box because she felt that, sooner or later, he would be hurt permanently. Besides, she could see no future for a man in the sports world, especially if all that a fellow got for winning was a gold watch or a trophy. To her, boxing was brawling, no matter how or where it was done. She wished he would find other outlets for his energy.

But the brawling instinct was not to be denied. One Friday night Jimmy and a group of friends got involved in a small riot outside a dance hall. Someone called the police, and as fists flew and girls screamed, both groups were surrounded and hustled off to the stationhouse.

When Mrs. Doolittle was notified by the police sergeant that her son was in jail, she decided that the time had come for Jimmy to learn a valuable lesson. "Keep him there until Monday morning," she said. "I'll come get him in time for school."

Losing his freedom, even temporarily, was a good lesson. The iron bars, the clanging of the cell doors, eating jail house meals and losing the right to come and go as he pleased, left their marks. He vowed never again to be caught up in a situation where his emotions would get the better of his reason. And he promised himself that he would never knowingly break the law so that he might be deprived of the precious gift of freedom—a freedom he didn't realize he had until he had lost it.

The brief jail experience and the discussion he had with his mother afterwards caused Jimmy to consider other ways to use his hands. He had come across some copies of *Popular Mechanics* magazine that featured then, as it still does, many do-it-yourself projects. He had seen an airplane for the first time in January 1910 at the first air meet ever held in the West. And now *Popular Mechanics* told its readers that anyone could make a glider just as the Wright brothers had done almost a decade before. Once a person had mastered the glider, he could, like the Wrights, attach a gasoline engine to it and never again have to count on wind gusts and updrafts to stay aloft.

The thought of making and flying his own glider took hold of Jimmy's mind and wouldn't let go. He knew how to handle tools fairly well as the result of his high school shop courses and the directions in the magazine were easy to follow. Working alone in a shed at the rear of his home, Jimmy's dream gradually progressed from drawings to reality. He spent hours fashioning the spruce wood strips into a pair of wings, covering them with cloth, and, piece by piece, putting the contraption together.

When the day came to test his creation, Jimmy carried it to a hill a few blocks away where the road to San Pedro had been cut through. The street was thirty feet below the hill and he figured that if he would take a running leap from the top he would glide smoothly to a soft landing some distance down the road. He didn't. Instead of soaring, he dropped. One wing of the glider collapsed, sending Jimmy to the bottom of the cut amidst a collection of wood, wire, and torn cloth. He was scratched and bruised but, worse yet, his pride had been injured because he had failed. Where had he gone wrong? He had followed the directions carefully. What mistakes had he made?

Jimmy dragged the wreckage home and spent the next few days carefully rebuilding it. What he needed, he decided, was more speed in order to get off the ground. When the glider was patched, he persuaded a friend to get his family car to give it take-off momentum. Jimmy tied a rope to the rear bumper and when he gave the signal, his friend started forward. Jimmy started to run behind the auto with the glider under his arms and when he thought he had enough speed he leaped into the air, fully expecting to be airborne like a kite that has finally caught the wind.

But, like a kite that has *not* caught the wind, Jimmy and his glider left the ground only briefly and then smashed to the roadway. His friend in the car could not stop very easily and dragged the helpless aeronaut and his flying machine a hundred feet or so. What the original crash did not do, the extra dragging did. Jimmy's clothes were torn, he was cut and bruised, and this time the glider was ripped to shreds.

Before he could build another glider, a new issue of *Popular Mechanics* arrived carrying detailed plans for a plane flown by the famous aeronaut Alberto Santos-Dumont, a Brazilian who had become an international hero in France. The plane was a 250-pound monoplane, called the *Demoiselle*, which was powered by a 30-horsepower gasoline engine.

Jimmy studied the Santos-Dumont drawings carefully and concluded that he had failed to soar in his glider because he couldn't run fast enough off the top of the hill or behind the auto. The *Demoiselle* had only one wing and the engine had provided all the power that was needed. He decided to rebuild his glider with only one wing. For the engine, he would use a second-hand motorcycle engine.

Rebuilding the glider proved to be an easy task. But getting the money to buy even a used motorcycle engine would take some doing. The only way to do it was with his fists. Although he was an amateur boxer there was a way to make money without being paid directly. It was the custom to give a gold watch to the winner of each match. The promoters of the matches would nearly always buy the watches back for ten dollars each.

Jimmy entered the weekly matches in downtown Los Angeles under an assumed name three weeks in a row and won each time. The accumulated thirty dollars equaled the price of the engine he wanted. He quickly set to work on his own version of the *Demoiselle*. The night before he planned to make his first flight, however, a thunderstorm slashed through Los Angeles and caught Jimmy's machine as it rested in his back yard. The revised glider did soar this time—right out of the Doolittle yard and over several neighbors' fences until it smashed to the ground in a confused pile of cloth, spruce splinters, and piano wire.

The mishap proved to be a good thing for American aviation. Years later, after Doolittle had studied aerodynamics in college, he discovered that his design had violated some of the basic principles of flight. While he might have been able to get his craft into the air briefly, the machine would have been incapable of sustained, safe flight. If he had gotten more than a few feet off the ground, he would have surely crashed, with every chance of killing himself.

The significance of the torn-up motorized glider was not lost on Mrs. Doolittle. She didn't like the thought of her only child being hurt boxing and the possibility that he might kill himself in a homemade flying machine. When Jimmy gathered up the pieces of his plane and brought them home, she knew what a blow it was to his young ego. She had known all along from the puffed lips and black eyes how he had earned the money for the motorcycle engine. "If you'll give up boxing and flying," she said, "I'll buy you a motorcycle."

Jimmy was elated. By this time he had just about decided there was no future in amateur boxing and since his version of an airplane was now nothing but a wreck, he agreed.

The motorcycle satisfied the restless energies of the boy in those years as his body and mind were struggling to become a man. He spent hours tinkering with the engine, shining the framework and zooming around Los Angeles. By this time he had fallen in love with a pretty girl with a broad smile, a happy disposition, and a Southern accent named Josephine Daniels. She had come from Louisiana with her parents and had retained the unhurried, calm demeanor that was characteristic of cultured families of the Old South.

But Jo Daniels puzzled Jimmy. She seemed completely unimpressed with his motorcycle, his boxing prowess, or his interest in flying. What frustrated him was that there wasn't anyone he could fight to win her over. If there had been a rival, he could just challenge him to a match, beat him to a pulp, and win his prize. But life in a world that included women was not that simple. Jo Daniels wanted her boy friend to be, first of all, a gentleman. Gentlemen did not go around looking for fights. They would, however, defend a lady's honor if it were impugned.

Jo Daniels changed Jimmy Doolittle. He began to wear a tie and comb his hair. He became conscious of his clothes and careful of his speech. He also became aware of how much money it took to go out on dates and buy gasoline for his motorcycle. He decided that he would turn to professional boxing for the money. However, to conceal his return to the ring from both his mother and Jo, he had to fight under an assumed name.

Although he was only a junior in high school, the cocky youngster looked older than his contemporaries and the boxing promoters liked his aggressive style. On weekends he cycled up and down the coast from Los Angeles making all the fight clubs that were so popular before World War I. Although Jimmy was small, he was solidly built and when he landed a punch, his opponent was usually rocked back on his heels. Invariably, it seemed, the men he fought were taller and had a longer reach. Jimmy made up for this difference with a furious, relentless attack that either flattened his opponent or caused the referee to stop the fight.

The fans, eager to root for an underdog, liked to see the little fighter win and Jimmy was able to get as much as $30 a bout. But the winning streak eventually came to an end. One night Doolittle was matched with a ring-wise veteran who fought under the name of "Spider" Kelly. A few seconds after they touched gloves at the start of the match, Jimmy knew that Kelly was an experienced professional. Instead of melting under Jimmy's hot-paced attack, Kelly danced neatly away, only to return with some jolting right-hand blows to the body that stung and rocked the young lad badly. Kelly feinted beautifully and led Jimmy into dropping his guard momentarily. The result was a series of powerful blows to the head that eventually cost Jimmy the fight. That night, reflecting on the experience, he knew he had learned another valuable lesson: No matter how good you might be in sports, someone will eventually come along who is better.

Jo Daniels did not like Jimmy to fight and told him so. She did not ask him to give it up but the message was clear because she refused to go see him box and did not even want to talk about it.

"Will you marry me?" Jimmy asked her suddenly one day during his senior year at Manual Arts High.

"You must think I'm out of my mind," she replied, indignantly. "I'd never marry a man who wants to fight all the time!"

"I'll give up fighting," he announced. "I'm going to Alaska after school's out and get a job. As soon as I have some money, I'll send for you."

Secretly pleased but concerned about what her mother would say to marriage at such an early age and living in far-off Alaska, Jo said, "My mother would never approve."

"I'm going to marry you, not your mother," he countered.

Jimmy did go to Alaska but it was no longer the land of opportunity that he thought it would be. Finding no job of any kind, he signed on a Los Angeles-bound ship as a steward and returned to face his sweetheart with the announcement that "We'll just have to wait a while."

"I never said I'd marry you—no matter what," she replied. "I think you should go to college and learn how to make a living before you ask a girl to be your wife."

Taking Jo's advice, Jimmy entered Los Angeles Junior College that fall and enrolled in engineering courses. During the next two years, he surprised himself and developed a liking for the math and science courses he was required to take and decided to enroll at the University of California to work toward a degree in mining engineering. In his spare time, he took up gymnastics and became very adept on the horizontal bar and parallel bars. Weighing a compact 130 pounds spread over a five-foot, six-inch frame now, he spent many hours working out alone or with several friends. Although he didn't realize it, he was developing a sense of balance, timing and self-discipline that would one day make him world famous—but not as an acrobat.

Although he had tried to forget boxing, the desire for physical combat was still strong. One day in the University of California gym, one of his friends told Jimmy that the boxing coach was holding elimination bouts in the 165-pound class to see who would represent their college against arch-rival Stanford. There were three contenders left now and Doolittle looked them over.

"You've done some boxing, Doolittle," one of his friends said, half joking. "Why don't you take those three guys on and you be the one to fight the Stanford man. They're bigger and heavier than you are but that means they're slower. Why don't you challenge them?"

"Believe I will," Jimmy said, matter-of-factly. "They don't look so tough."

While his friends watched, Doolittle approached the coach, Marcus Freed, and asked if he could try out for the team.

"Those fellows have thirty pounds on you," Freed replied. "They're middleweights. Besides, they've all got more reach than you have."

"That doesn't bother me," Jimmy said, "so it shouldn't bother them."

Freed shrugged, helped Doolittle on with his gloves, and chose one of the three middleweights who was about four inches taller than Doolittle.

At the sound of the bell, the two young men, looking like Mutt and Jeff, rushed to the center of the ring, touched gloves, and backed off. The tall lad pushed out at Doolittle with his left glove as if to flick off a bug that was bothering him. It was the only gesture he was able to make. Doolittle zapped his own left hand to his opponent's mid-section and ducked under the dangling left arm with a sledgehammer right hand to the chin. The taller fighter was paralyzed and dropped to the canvas like a bag of wet sand. It took five minutes to bring him around.

Coach Freed was amazed. In all his years of coaching he had never seen such speed and power come from a lightweight fighter.

"You've fought somewhere before," he said. "Want to take on the next man?"

Doolittle nodded. By the end of the round, the second middleweight had gone the way of the first.

"That's enough for today," Freed announced. "Be back here tomorrow if you want to take the third man on. He's had more experience than the other two."

By the next day, word about the two knockouts had spread rapidly all across the sprawling campus. By bout time, the gym was full of spectators all wanting to see David fight Goliath.

As Doolittle quickly discovered, the third middleweight was much better than the first two. Having watched the furious assault Doolittle had made on his teammates and mindful of the power in those smaller fists, he held Jimmy off with a long left hand. Try as he might, Doolittle couldn't get in close. He danced around the taller man, flinging rapid left and right jabs and looking for an opening. By the end of the round, Doolittle was winded and realized that he had to finish his opponent off fast. Not having boxed for a long time, he was not in the best of shape for three-minute rounds. He knew there was only one way for him to win this bout.

At the bell, Doolittle shot out of his corner like a locomotive coming full speed out of a tunnel. He began throwing punches with the fury of a maddened hornet going after someone who had just knocked down its nest. The tall lad was stunned by the onslaught. He put up his guard feebly but the hornet's stings could not be avoided. His guard dropped, a hard right landed on his chin, and he sagged face down onto the campus. With that one punch, Doolittle, the lightweight, had become middleweight boxing champion of the University of California!

Although Jimmy had won three bouts without practice, he knew that he was out of shape because he had been winded by the effort. With the Stanford match only a week away, he had a lot of training to do. Following Coach Freed's instructions, he went on a regimen of running and bag punching for the next seven days. By the day of the match, Doolittle felt confident that he could win.

Before the bout, Freed cautioned Doolittle about his defense. "You can hit well," he said, "but a good boxer with longer arms will wear you down and then blast you when you let your defense drop. Your best bet is to do what you did on the first two fights—get in there fast and explode!"

Doolittle knew the coach was right, especially when he saw his Stanford opponent climb into the ring. Tall, lanky, and assured, he smiled at his short opponent across the ring as if to say, "This won't take long."

Doolittle's resolve began to build. He would wipe that smile off in a hurry, he told himself. He glowered at his opponent while the referee gave them instructions and felt a sudden rage sweep over him. That smile had to go!

When the bell rang, Doolittle burst out of his corner and aimed a right at the smile that lurked continually on the tall man's face. The right didn't land but was quickly blocked. Doolittle countered and the two exchanged a flurry of blows. The long left arm of his opponent fended off Jimmy's blows masterfully. The smile was still there mocking each attempt to get through the defense.

Doolittle slowed his attack and began a series of feints and dodges. That smile irked him; he had to get rid of it. Finally, there was an opening and Doolittle's strong right blasted under that long left arm and landed on target. The Stanford man sagged and fell. The fight was over.

In the locker room sometime later, his opponent revived, arose, and headed toward Jimmy, hand outstretched and with that same smile covering his face.

"That was a good punch," he said, earnestly. "Congratulations!"

Doolittle was surprised. He suddenly felt ashamed of himself for almost hating the man because of his smile. "It was a lucky one," he said, apologetically.

"Nonsense," the man replied, still smiling. "You deserved to win with a right like that!"

Jimmy never forgot this remark or the man who made it. His name was Eric Pedley, who later became a noted polo player. Pedley and his smile had taught Jimmy another valuable lesson—a lesson about sportsmanship and sincerity.

4. The Course Is Set

ALTHOUGH HE DIDN'T REALIZE it at the time, Jimmy Doolittle had almost grown up with heavier-than-air aviation. He was born in 1896 and a number of men had already been conducting experiments for six years trying to mate a glider with an engine. Professor Samuel P. Langley, secretary of the Smithsonian Institution, was one of the first Americans to encourage such experiments. He constructed a steam-driven model airplane in 1890 but it was unsuccessful. Two years later, he built two models with carbonic-acid gas and air engines but they also failed to fly. He built six more models powered by small steam engines that were not successful. On May 6, 1896, seven months before Jimmy was born, a tiny, unmanned model, sixteen feet long with a thirteen-foot wingspread, finally flew for a half mile over the Potomac River. Powered by a small 1½-horsepower steam engine, it was launched from a catapult mounted atop a houseboat. Another flight was made on November 28. Based on these successes, two years later the War Department awarded Dr. Langley a $50,000 contract to construct a man-carrying version that he called his *Aerodrome A*.

It took five years for Dr. Langley to construct the craft in the

Smithsonian shops. Finally, on October 7, 1903, Charles M. Manly, a mechanic hired by Langley, tried to fly it from the top of the houseboat. He didn't and nearly drowned before he and the machine were fished out of the Potomac.

Manly tried again on December 8 and failed again. An army officer who had observed both attempts reported to his superiors that "The claim that an engine-driven, man-carrying aerodrome has been constructed lacks the proof which actual flight alone can give."

On December 17, 1903—three days after Jimmy Doolittle's seventh birthday—two obscure bicycle repairmen from Dayton, Ohio, without benefit of subsidy, made history's first sustained, controlled, power-driven flight in a heavier-than-air machine. Orville and Wilbur Wright, who had never studied science or mechanics and had never been to college, succeeded where others had failed.

When Jimmy was 12 years old, the Wrights sold *Aeroplane No. 1* to the Aeronautical Division, U.S. Army's Signal Corps, and the nation's air force was born. By the time Jimmy had tried to fly his first glider in 1912, at the age of fifteen, world heavier-than-air aviation had come a long way, considering its slow start. Speed had increased to more than 80 miles an hour; distances of 400 miles had been spanned without interim landings; the heavier-than-air endurance record was now 14 hours; altitudes of 13,000 feet had been reached, and the number of passengers successfully carried on one flight had increased to 12. The hydroplane had been developed; the first landing on the deck of a ship had been made, and the first successful catapult launchings were conducted.

Ironically, by the time World War I began in Europe (1914), the United States was far behind several European nations in aviation. The native land of the Wright brothers had only purchased a total of 24 planes for its air force, of which 10 had been destroyed by accidents. In contrast, France had 1,500 army and 1,000 private planes; Germany had 1,000 army and 450 private planes; England had about 100 planes.

In the early days of the war, the airplane was not used to drop

This historic photograph was taken at Kitty Hawk, North Carolina, on December 17, 1903. It is the first successful flight by man ever made in a heavier-than-air flying machine. Orville Wright is at the controls as elder brother Wilbur observes.

The Curtiss *Jenny* training plane was used to chase guerrilla bands under the leadership of Pancho Villa. Commander of the First Aero Squadron was Capt. (later Maj. Gen.) Benjamin D. Foulois, shown here with one of the *Jennies* he used in the first combat air action by United States flying forces.

bombs or spew machine gun bullets into enemy planes. It was used as the eyes of the army on the ground. The early reconnaissance planes went up unarmed, usually carrying a pilot and an observer. Planes of both sides flew unhindered back and forth across the front lines; pilots waved at each other as they passed.

It wasn't long before things changed, however. Observers riding in the rear seats took pot shots at enemy planes with rifles. Soon swiveling machine guns were installed and the observer became a gunner. Then the French figured out how to mount machine guns in front of the pilot so that he, too, could fire at an adversary. The airplane then quickly became a flying gun platform as single-seat "pursuit" planes began playing a deadly game of aerial hide-and-seek.

As the planes became weapons, they also became faster, heavier, and stronger. They began to carry bombs, which were dropped on enemy supply depots and ammunition dumps. They were not American planes, however. In spite of the fact that France, Russia, England, Germany, and Italy were spending millions annually on aviation, the United States had earmarked only a few thousand dollars for airplanes.

In 1916, Francisco "Pancho" Villa, a Mexican bandit, raided Columbus, New Mexico, and killed a number of Americans. The American Army was ordered to send a "punitive expedition" across the border to chase him down. The First Aero Squadron, consisting of eight Curtiss JN-3 *Jenny* scout planes, that had seen strenuous service in Oklahoma and Texas, accompanied General John J. Pershing's forces as a reconnaissance unit. It was the only combat air squadron the country had.

The sad state of American aviation quickly became apparent as the eight planes, immediately reduced to six by accidents, tried to follow Pershing's forces. The under-powered *Jennies* couldn't climb high enough to search the mountainous areas where Villa's troops were hiding. The dry climate warped the plane's propellers and the blowing sand wreaked havoc with the engines. Within a few weeks, Captain Benjamin D. Foulois, the squadron commander, made the following report to his superiors:

The six aeroplanes now in use have been subjected, for nearly ten months, to severe weather conditions in Oklahoma and Texas, exposed to rain, high winds and severe cold weather conditions.

As a result of these months of field service, all aeroplanes have been subject to severe wear and tear. With the present extreme field service conditions every machine is liable, at any day, to be placed out of commission as unfit and too dangerous for further field service.

These aeroplanes are not capable of meeting present military needs incident to this expedition. Their low power motors and limited climbing ability with the necessary military load makes it impossible to safely operate any one of these machines in the vicinity of the mountains which cover the present theater of operations.

Foulois pleaded for "At least ten of the highest powered, highest climbing and best weight carrying aeroplanes" that the government could obtain. They were not to be had.

Although the United States had achieved the distinction of owning the world's first military airplane in 1909, it practically stood still in aviation development during the next few years compared to other nations. By 1916, the total government appropriations spent on military aviation was only $600,000—not enough to sustain an industry and encourage aircraft development for national defense. The aircraft industry, what there was of it, was kept alive mainly by civilian support.

During these lean years, the Aero Club of America (now the National Aeronautic Association), not the government, was the main organization in arousing public interest and developing an air force. Through its efforts, the Aero Club succeeded in pushing Congress to increase appropriations for military aviation and fostered the training of several hundred civilian pilots who were later absorbed into the Aviation Officers Reserve Corps.

Three months after the United States declared war on Germany in 1917, a bill appropriating $640 million for military aviation was finally passed. Supposedly, the United States could now build thousands of planes and train hundreds of pilots to win the war in the air. But air power takes time to build and the task that faced a country without any semblance of an aircraft industry was so difficult as to be almost impossible.

While American industry tried to meet the demand for thousands of military planes, the call went out to the nation's youth to volunteer for service with the army's expanding air arm. The aerial exploits of the "name" foreign aviators fighting in European skies who had become "aces" because they had shot down five or more enemy planes fired the imagination of the country's young men. Thousands of young American men applied. Then, as now, the problem became one of selecting the right kind of men to be military pilots.

Army recruiting sergeants throughout the country were given instructions to reject anyone not meeting the pilot criteria. A War Department order explained what these criteria were:

> The candidate should be naturally athletic and have a reputation of reliability, punctuality and honesty. He should have a cool head in emergencies, good eye for distance, keen ear for familiar sounds, steady hands and sound body with plenty of reserve; he should be quick-witted, highly intelligent and tractable. Immature, high-strung, over-confident, impatient candidates are not desired.

Successful applicants were sent to ground schools set up at eight large engineering colleges across the country. During an intensive eight-week course, students were instructed in theory of flight, principles of radio, code, aerial photography, meteorology, map reading, gunnery, aircraft engines, and aerial tactics.

After ground school, cadets were trained at one of eighteen flying fields that were hurriedly constructed or leased from private owners. Each pilot trainee stayed at these fields from six weeks to two months, depending upon his individual ability to absorb the instruction. The flying course was divided into three phases: dual instruction, solo practice, and cross-country flying. An official Air Force history* described the training this way:

> First was the dual work in which the cadet went up into the air with the instructor and was given an opportunity to accustom himself to the feel of the plane. At the start he was largely a passenger,

* Sweetser, Arthur, *The American Air Service*, p. 110–113.

now and again, however, operating the controls as the instructor started, landed, or swept about the field at an altitude of about 500 feet. As rapidly as his skill warranted, he was given charge of the machine until he was able to get it up, down, and around with safety. All this time he was encouraged to advance, and at the same time he was protected against worry or nervousness by having impressed upon him the naturalness and simplicity of the whole performance.

After from four to nine hours of this work came the second stage, when the cadet first went into the air alone. At the start he repeated each phase of his dual work, and then he began to extend it until he was making figure eights at a 45-degree angle and gliding down with motor throttled from about 1,500 feet towards a previously designated mark. Next he was taught to make accurate turns with the banks approaching the vertical, to climb steeply to the verge of a stall, and to land in a very small circle. All of this work required another 24 hours in the air. All through the solo work the cadet was directed with great detail. Before each flight he received exact instructions as to the evolutions, altitude and landing places, and after each flight he reported to the instructors for criticism. Never was more than two hours of flying a day allowed to any cadet, nor could flights be less than 20 or more than 40 minutes in length. Occasionally the instructor went up during this part of the training to correct any bad form that might have developed. At the end of this solo work the cadet was master of the plane for simple flying over a prescribed field.

As the final step in this primary training came the cross-country work, beginning with a flight around a triangle 10 miles to a side, to give familiarity with prominent landmarks. Three flights, each 30 miles out and 30 miles back, then followed, at altitudes of at least 2,000 feet, the cadet receiving detailed instructions as to routes, landing places, and map. As much instruction in compass work and map reading was given as was possible with the number of planes on hand.

. . . After the 60-mile cross-country flight and an altitude test of 10,000 feet, the cadet was considered to have passed his reserve military aviation requirements, which gave him his commission and the right to wear his wings. He was now skilled in all ordinary flying and was ready to go on to the advanced schools for acrobatics and specialized training for war work.

When Jimmy Doolittle had completed his second year at Los Angeles Junior College in 1916, he was convinced that he wanted to be a mining engineer. After enrolling at the University of California, he had begun to take his future seriously.

But no young man in those days was immune to what was happening in the air in Europe. Newspapers and magazines glorified the great airmen whose feats in the skies of Europe quickly became legendary. Names like Von Richthofen, Bishop, Fonck, Guynemer, Udet, and Mannock were well known to every American lad long before the United States became involved. The idea of men fighting alone, pitting their skills against each other thousands of feet above the earth, fired young imaginations. Stories of dogfights, flying circus forays, and speedy new pursuit planes were magnified and gained more glamour as they were embellished and retold in adventure magazines.

Jimmy Doolittle, caught up in the excitement of the times, thought he could qualify for pilot training and enlisted in the Signal Corps Reserve, Aviation Section, in the summer of 1917. Instead of going to flying school, however, he was told to go home and wait for orders. They finally came in the fall and he found himself taking preflight training at the University of California, his alma mater.

Jimmy chafed at the many hours spent marching on the drill field but told himself that it was a necessary evil. The courses on military justice, personal health, and administration were worthwhile, but he was anxious to get in the air. He was afraid the war would be over before he could.

Jimmy was also afraid that he would lose his girl friend, too, if he didn't do something about it. When the announcement was made that the flying cadets would be granted a Christmas leave, he made up his mind. During his time off, he was going to marry Jo Daniels and make her Mrs. Doolittle.

Jo's mother did not favor the idea of her daughter marrying a boxer and she was positive that she didn't want a flier as a son-in-law—especially one who hadn't yet finished his training and was making only about $60 a month.

Jimmy didn't care what Jo's mother thought. "As I told you before, I want to marry you, Jo, not your mother," he said when he told her his plan. On Christmas Eve, 1917, the two young people went to Los Angeles City Hall and were married just before the clerks closed their offices. Jo paid for the license with a five-dollar bill her mother had given her for a Christmas present. Between them the newly-married couple had less than twenty dollars for a honeymoon but they drove to San Diego and survived the next few days by eating at cafeterias where servicemen and their wives or girl friends were served free meals. By the time Jimmy dropped Jo off at her house in Los Angeles and returned to the university, they had about twenty-five cents between them.

In January 1918, Jimmy was ordered to begin flight training at Rockwell Field near San Diego. He was assigned to a civilian instructor named Charlie Todd, a lean, tanned man whose job it was to give flying instruction and also to evaluate the young men on the ground as well as in the cockpit. Todd wondered about this scrappy little fellow barely tall enough to pass the physical. He seemed alert and well-coordinated enough and intent upon becoming a flying officer. But could so short a man fly an airplane well, especially when he could barely see over the side of the cockpit?

Instructor Todd gave Jimmy eight hours of flying instruction in a Curtiss JN-4 *Jenny,* the minimum time before a student was allowed to solo. But Todd hesitated to let his student solo and Jimmy himself wondered whether or not he could fly alone.

As Todd and Jimmy taxied out to takeoff position for one more dual flight, they heard a thunderous crash a few feet away. Startled, they looked up to see a cloud of dust and a pile of splintered wood and torn fabric just ahead of them. Before they could react, there was another crash near the first. Todd shut off the engine and he and Jimmy ran to the wreckage.

They quickly realized what had happened. Two training planes had collided while coming in for landings. Both had lost control and plunged onto the end of the landing area. Todd and Jimmy tore through the mangled cockpits of both planes and pulled the four men out. One instructor pilot was dead; the other instructor and one student were badly injured.

The crashes had unnerved Jimmy and the doubts about his

own adequacy returned. Todd sensed this and made a quick decision.

"Doolittle, you still want to fly?" he asked, as the ambulances departed and they walked back to their plane.

The answer came out before Jimmy realized he had said it. "Yes, sir," he replied.

"All right. Get back in and take it up for an hour—alone."

Before he had time to analyze his feelings, Jimmy taxied out to takeoff position, ran up his engine and was soon off the ground. The next hour was the most exhilarating he had ever known. He dived and zoomed and shouted at the top of his lungs with happiness. He was master of a flying machine! All doubts about his ability to fly vanished and his future course in life was set from that hour on.

While Jimmy was at Rockwell, Jo had obtained a job at a shipyard where secretaries were badly needed for the seven-day work weeks that war had brought. While her new husband continued with his training, she did not realize that her future was also being determined in the sky over San Diego. She soon realized that Jimmy loved flying and that she would probably have to share him with an airplane while he was in the army, but she didn't mind. She felt sure that her restless, daredevil husband would never be content with army life and its discipline. As soon as the war was over, he would surely want to return to the university, get his degree, and become a mining engineer.

But Jo Doolittle's husband had other ideas which became more firmly entrenched with each minute he spent in the air. After he graduated, he was going to see to it that the army sent him to Europe to fight in the air. There was a war on and he wasn't going to miss it!

The plans each of them had eventually came about in one form or another. But it would be a quarter of a century before Jimmy Doolittle would realize his dream of fighting an enemy of his country in the air. By that time, he would have obtained a doctorate in a new kind of engineering that emerged from World War I—aeronautical science.

5. More Confidence than Skill

MOST EXPERIENCED FLIERS ACKNOWLEDGE that the most dangerous time in a military pilot's life is between the time he has graduated from flying school and when he has amassed about one thousand hours of flying time. This is the period when a young pilot has more confidence in his skill than he should. It is usually during this time that he will attempt maneuvers in an airplane without leaving any margin for his lack of skill or that the airplane is not built to withstand.

Jimmy Doolittle entered this pilot's "danger period" on March 11, 1918, when he received the silver wings of an Army Air Service pilot and the gold bars of a second lieutenant. He had about two hundred hours flying time and was itching to get to France and fly the fast pursuit planes of the day—the French *Spads* and *Nieuports* or the British *Sopwith Camels*.

His desire to get into combat was not to be realized. Instead of going to an East Coast embarkation point, his first orders as a new pilot sent him to Camp Dick, Texas. This assignment might have been worthwhile except that there were no airplanes there and none were expected.

Doolittle was furious, but he was not alone. Several of his

classmates had been sent there, also. All were assigned routine duties training ground troops in personal sanitation, marching, and administration. At day's end, the displaced pilots would get together and scheme ways to get to France. As the warm spring days turned to a typically hot Texas summer, the young lieutenants became extremely frustrated but helpless to convince anyone in the army hierarchy that they should have been shipped elsewhere.

Just as all hope seemed gone that he would ever see an airplane again, Jimmy received orders to report to Wright Field, Ohio, where he took courses in aircraft and engine maintenance and got a few hours of flying in. From there he was sent to Camp Dix, New Jersey, and now was sure he was going to go overseas. Instead, he was sent to Gertsner Field, Lake Charles, Louisiana, for advanced flight instruction.

"What are we going to fly here?" Doolittle asked.

"The Thomas-Morse," he was told. "Hottest airplane in the sky."

For its time, the American-built Thomas-Morse S-4C scout plane was an excellent airplane for training. It was more forgiving of mistakes than other single-seat pursuits and was relatively easy to handle. It was a sturdy machine, which made it excellent for aerobatics. However, it was tail heavy and ground-looped easily. Powered by LeRhone or Gnome engines which were lubricated by castor oil, the S-4C had no brakes and suffered many ground accidents. Added to this was the fact that the engine had no throttle—just an on-off switch so that it went either full throttle or not at all.

In spite of its shortcomings, Jimmy and his classmates liked the Thomas-Morse and felt sure they would soon be flying it against the Germans. But during the last week of their training at Gertsner, a hurricane slashed through Louisiana and the three hundred planes there were reduced to splinters. The field was practically wiped out. After many days helping to clean up the debris, Doolittle received orders to report back to Rockwell Field to be an instructor of cadets in the advanced training phase, which now included aerial gunnery.

Although the assignment was the perfect one for the energetic Doolittle, he chafed at being given the task of teaching others to fly rather than fighting in combat. But, as had become an ingrained characteristic now, he decided that if he had to be an instructor, he would be the best instructor in the U.S. Air Service. In order to teach others, he knew he had to be able to do every maneuver in the flying book—perfectly. As a result, he practiced many long hours perfecting loops, rolls, dives, and landings. When he heard of new maneuvers being used in France, he carefully worked them out in his head and then tried them out in the Thomas-Morse single-seaters or the two-seat Curtiss *Jennies.*

It wasn't long before Jimmy started to be known as a daredevil pilot who would try anything in the air. When he tired of the routine of student training, he teamed up with Lt. John McCulloch and the pair of them would practice wingwalking. While one flew, the other would climb out on a wing and do handstands or skin-the-cat on the axle that connected the landing wheels.

Since such stunts were against the rules, it was inevitable that Jimmy would be caught. It came about when Cecil B. DeMille, the famous movie maker, was at Rockwell shooting scenes for a forthcoming motion picture. As he was grinding away photographing landings and takeoffs, his eye caught a plane on final approach and he trained the camera on it. What made the sight different was that a man was calmly sitting underneath the fuselage between the wheels as the trainer approached and landed.

DeMille's camera followed the plane to its parking spot and recorded the passenger getting up and walking blithely away with the pilots, both laughing and entirely unaware that their unusual method of passenger carrying had been photographed. The next day, DeMille showed the film to Colonel Harvey Burwell, the field commander.

"I got some good shots of your pilots yesterday," DeMille said, "but there's one last scene here that I think you ought to see."

As Burwell watched, the sequence showing the man sitting between the wheels came on. Although the face of the man was not clearly discernible, Burwell jumped up, shouting, "That's Doolittle! I know it is!"

He turned to his executive officer and said, angrily, "Find Doolittle and ground him for a month!"

"But, sir, how do you know that's Doolittle?" the officer asked.

"He's the only pilot on the field that would have nerve enough to pull a stunt like that," Burwell replied. "Make him permanent officer of the day for a month. Maybe that'll teach him a lesson."

Jimmy, surprised that he had been caught, took his punishment, but didn't like it. Being officer of the day meant being on call for twenty-four hours at a time to respond to any incident that occurred on the field—from an automobile accident to an airplane crash. It was tiring enough for one full day, but a month of being on call at any and all hours was quite a punishment.

What made the punishment doubly difficult for Doolittle was that several instructors were chosen that month to make a cross-country flight from San Diego to New York and return. The pilots who went received considerable local publicity and one of them couldn't resist rubbing it in to Doolittle upon return. "Good experience, Doolittle," he said. " 'Course, I realize that you probably learned a lot more here on the ground working for good old Colonel Burwell."

Doolittle brooded about missing the trip and wondered what it proved. For several days he studied a map of the United States and a plan formed in his mind. Now back on flying status, he went to Colonel Burwell.

"Sir, I don't think we got the right kind of publicity out of that flight from San Diego to New York," he told his commanding officer.

"It was well planned and executed, Doolittle," Burwell said. "What do you think we could have done better?"

"Sir, the trip didn't prove anything to the American public," Jimmy answered. "If the flight had been from Rockwell Field to Bolling Field in Washington, D.C., it could have been publicized as proving that the airplane could be used as a fast army courier that could deliver secret messages from a far-flung installation to

War Department headquarters in the nation's capital. That angle would give your command better nationwide publicity as well as bring credit to the army."

Burwell was convinced. "Well, what do you recommend, Doolittle? That we try it again?"

"Yes, sir," Doolittle said, and began briefing his boss on the route he recommended be flown and the publicity plan that should be developed.

"And I suppose you think you're the man to lead it?" Burwell asked, with a note of sarcasm in his voice.

"Yes, sir," Doolittle answered.

"I agree," Burwell said, to Jimmy's surprise. "I'll let you have three Curtiss *Jennies*. I'll choose the two other pilots."

For the next few days Doolittle busied himself with preparations and briefed the other pilots, Walt Smith and Charlie Haynes. The trio took off early one morning and made the first stop at Indio, California, as planned, without incident. But the next day, nothing went as planned. The trio left Indio for Needles and arrived over the small desert town almost out of gas.

Doolittle and his two wingmen circled, looking for the airport that was supposed to be there. None of them could see anything but rock-filled desert. In desperation as the gas ran low, Doolittle decided to land on the highway just outside Needles. He made the approach and landed safely, as did Smith, but Haynes ran out of gas as he was getting ready to follow Smith down and made a dead stick landing in the desert. As he touched down, one wheel hit a rock and the plane ground-looped into a pile of wreckage. Fortunately, Haynes was not hurt.

Doolittle called his commanding officer at Rockwell and reported that they were at Needles on schedule.

"Any problems, Doolittle?" Burwell asked.

"Only one," Jimmy said. "We wrecked one plane. Haynes is O.K. Smith and I will go on." To Jimmy's relief, Burwell did not object.

After getting fueled up at a gas station, Doolittle took off and circled as Smith revved up to follow. As Jimmy watched, Smith ran down the road but hooked his wing on a telephone pole and ended up in a cloud of dust, unhurt and mad at himself for his bad luck. Doolittle promptly landed to see if Smith was all right. He called Colonel Burwell again to tell him what had happened.

"That's all, Doolittle," Burwell said, coldly. "Two out of three is too many. Come on back here before you kill yourself."

After arranging for the pilots and their wrecks to be returned to Rockwell, Doolittle took off next morning and ran into bad weather. The old *Jenny* wouldn't climb above it, so Jimmy dived underneath the clouds. He tried to identify his position but could see nothing on the ground that resembled the symbols on his map. The weather gradually got worse and Jimmy knew he had to land while he could. He picked out a freshly plowed field but it was a bad decision. As he leveled off, the wheels caught on the upturned earth and the plane promptly flipped over onto its back.

The mishap had occurred so fast that Jimmy didn't know what had happened. Fortunately, he was unhurt but got covered with oil as he dug his way out of the cockpit. As he scrambled clear, his pants caught on a piece of metal and he felt a sudden draft where the seat of his pants had been. He soon forgot it, though, as two farmers rushed up and offered to help him to right the plane and assess the damage.

Fortunately, the *Jenny* was not badly damaged. The three men turned it over and within about three hours, with the weather now improved, Doolittle had the *Jenny* on its way home after verifying that the engine was functioning smoothly and that he was where the farmers said he was on the map.

Doolittle landed safely at Rockwell Field, where he was met by the operations officer.

"Better get to the colonel's office right away," he said. "He's boiling mad."

Doolittle nodded and strode briskly into headquarters without realizing how he looked all covered with oil and with his uniform in shreds.

He reported to Colonel Burwell with a brisk salute and was met with a torrent of cuss words, several of which Doolittle had never heard before.

Jimmy took it stoically. When the colonel finally ran out of his extensive vocabulary, he said, "Yes, sir, you're perfectly right, sir. May I go now, sir?"

Burwell was purple from the effort he had expended during his tirade. "Doolittle, you're a damned Chinese Ace. Know what that is?" he bellowed.

Doolittle shook his head. "No, sir," he answered.

"That's a pilot who wrecks more of his own country's planes than he does of the enemy's. Understand?"

"Yes, sir," Jimmy replied, grinning. "May I go now, sir?"

"Yes, damn it. Go!"

Doolittle saluted and about-faced.

Burwell stared in disbelief at the retreating lieutenant whose whole backside was exposed to full view. "Hold it!" he shouted, livid with rage. "You dumb dodo! You don't even have sense enough to keep your butt in your pants! Get out of here before I put you in front of a court-martial!"

"Yes, sir," was all Doolittle could think to say as he bolted out the door.

Shortly after the Armistice ending World War I was signed in November 1918, a military air show was announced by the San Diego Chamber of Commerce. An "aerial parade" of more than two hundred warplanes was planned. The Los Angeles *Times* noted: "Nothing on so massive a scale as this flight will be has ever been attempted either in this country or Europe." The newspaper added, prophetically, that: "The Flight will probably be the last of its kind held in this country or Europe for many years . . . as the large permanent aeronautical institutions will be reduced to peace strengths within a short time."

The object of the air show and flyby was to show the public what their tax dollars had bought in the way of military air-power and to prove that American pilots were as good as the Europeans who had become household names. A large forma-tion, consisting of *Spads*, Thomas-Morse speed scouts, and Cur-tiss bombers and training planes, was scheduled. Following the mass flyby, combat pilots who had flown in Europe were to en-tertain the spectators with acrobatics and combat maneuvers.

The final act on the program was the performance of "five aerial gymnasts." Their leader was Jimmy Doolittle, selected after several days of intensive competition in which he proved himself to be the best stunt flier at Rockwell and its auxiliary fields. On November 24, 1918, the Los Angeles *Times* described the spectacle:

Promptly at 10 o'clock the comparatively slow-going Curtiss training planes left the ground at Rockwell Field and began to circle the island. Fifty of these got into the air and then an equal number of fast two-seaters rose and started to trail them. Then forty of the spidery Thomas-Morse scouts took the air and the huge squadron moved over Point Loma, gradually working into the form of a huge V, which we all know stands for Victory.

Meanwhile from East and Ream Fields, the two subsidiary training plants, seventy more fast machines preceded by five star stunt artists climbed to get into the aerial swim. Soon the 210 fast planes were swarming over North Island like so many bees and being herded into formation by the fifteen leaders who conversed with one another through the air by telephone quite as casually as you and I pass the time of day!

By 11 o'clock the formation was complete, and with the quintet of daring acrobats the greatest fleet of airplanes ever assembled in this country proceeded to write victory in the sky while thousands of spectators in the streets and on housetops cheered themselves hoarse, their excited shrieks and yells completely drowned by the shattering roar of the mighty motors.

So close to one another that they seemed almost to touch, they formed a ceiling over the city that almost blotted out the struggling rays of the sun and with majestic solemnity they patrolled the air, magnificent in the perfection of their formation, and while they formed a perfect background at 5,000 feet, the five acrobats below swooped, dived, looped, and spun in as perfect unison as though they had been operated by a single hand.

For nearly an hour the great parade moved across the clouds and then slowly and almost imperceptively the ranks began to thin out as in splendidly planned order the planes went home to roost in their North Island hangars. And as the numbers decreased, the antics and evolutions of the five stunt men increased until finally the skies cleared and the acrobats held the center of the heavens alone, supreme in the mad glory of their thrilling feats.

. . . The five daring acrobats whose daring skill provided the chief thrill of the day were Lts. D. W. Watkins, H. H. Bass, J. H. Doolittle, W. S. Smith, and H. O. Williams, all of Ream Field, who won the right to form the stunt squad in open competition from a score of pilots.

The competition and the thrill of winning it had whetted Doolittle's appetite for still more flying. He had found that he could compete in the skies and win, just as he had done in the ring. He practiced acrobatics for many hours after first analyzing every maneuver on the ground. He gradually found out what the limitations of his plane were and his own limitations as well. He slowly built his skill to meet those limitations—something many other pilots did not take the time to do. By the time he strapped himself in the cockpit, he was far better equipped mentally for "aerial gymnastics" than his fellow pilots. His success proved to Jimmy that this methodical, scientific approach to flying would get results. He had won this competition. He was determined that he would win others.

Jimmy stayed at the San Diego base for about six months, then was transferred, first to the 104th Aero Squadron at Kelly Field, Texas, and then to Eagle Pass on the Mexican border, where he joined the 90th Aero Squadron. It was the 90th's job to patrol the border and protect American towns from occasional raids by Mexican bandits, spot illegal border crossers, and prevent smuggling.

By the end of 1919, the Army Air Service had been reduced to a few hundred pilots and about as many planes. The country was tired of war and anything connected with it. Planes were sold by the hundreds to pilots who used them to barnstorm around the country and try to make a living using the flying skills they had learned to fight a war in the air. Some gave hops to passengers from farmers' fields; others took up stunt flying at county fairs. Some tried to start small airlines. A few joined the Air Mail Service that had been started by army pilots in May, 1918, and was beginning to expand across the country with civilian pilots.

Jimmy Doolittle decided to stay with the army, although he thought the job of flying border patrol was dull and much too routine. He used the time wisely, however. He flew as often as he could and learned something new on each flight. He tried new maneuvers and techniques and was constantly testing his own stamina and ability to withstand G-forces. He stored up knowledge for future use—knowledge that he hoped would all be put together someday in the future.

Jimmy remained at Eagle Pass for about a year, then was transferred back to Kelly Field for assignment to the Air Service Mechanical School. It was a welcome opportunity, in his view, because it gave him the chance to tinker and experiment with engines and planes. Since he already had had some engineering at the University of California, he was able to apply some of the knowledge he had gained to his new job. He experimented with gasolines and lubricants, propellers, and weight and balance changes. He began to wonder how far an airplane could go if it had enough gas on board. Then, one day, he got an idea. Why not take an old De Havilland DH-4 two-seat training plane, put gas tanks in that extra seat space and try to set a new speed record for flying coast-to-coast?

The more he thought about it, the more he wanted to try it. The first man ever to fly across the United States was Calbraith P. Rodgers, who had made the trip from New York to Pasadena in 1911 in spite of 19 crashes en route, the last of which caused him to fly the final few miles with one leg in a cast. It had taken Rodgers 49 days to make the trip. His longest single flight was only 133 miles.

Others had tried to beat Rodgers' record but none had succeeded. The idea of competing against a record as old as Rodgers' intrigued Jimmy and he studied the reasons why Army Lt. Alex Pearson and others had failed. According to his calculations, a DH-4 could be outfitted with sufficient gas tanks so that only one refueling stop would be required between Pablo Beach, Florida, and San Diego—the route he chose to fly. Furthermore, if his engine held out and fatigue did not get the better of him, he thought he could make the flight in less than twenty-four hours.

Jimmy carefully set down his plan in writing and asked for official permission to try for the record. If he succeeded, it would look good for the Air Service. If he failed, well, it wouldn't be because it wasn't theoretically possible.

Before he could carry out his plans, Jimmy was ordered to Langley Field, Virginia, to participate in bombing tests dreamed up by the famous General Billy Mitchell who had become a most controversial figure because of his views about the value of the airplane as a military weapon. Mitchell had incurred the wrath of the U.S. Navy admirals by saying, "They are too stupid to face the fact that sea power is done for. They don't know it but battleships are obsolete. They can be sunk easily by bombs from an airplane. And the airplane doesn't even have to hit the battleship to sink it!"

Such a statement was considered completely irrational in those days when U.S. Navy ships were considered the toughest in the world and when airplanes were not yet accepted as much more than useful for observation purposes. Some said airplanes should never attempt to fly outside sight of land for fear of getting lost; others said that bombs big enough to sink a battleship could never be lifted by any airplane that could ever be built.

Billy Mitchell pleaded for the chance to prove his theories of airpower and took his case to the public through his writings and appearances before congressional committees. He told one group of congressmen that he could prove what he said if he could be allowed to have several captured German warships, including the giant battleship, *Ostfriesland,* for tests.

The idea was so preposterous to navy officials that former Secretary of the Navy Josephus Daniels declared that he would stand bareheaded on the deck of any battleship and let Mitchell's bombers have their fun. He told the press he was confident that he would, "By God, expect to remain safe."

The Navy, not as sure as Daniels, fought the idea and tried to have political pressure brought to bear to prevent Mitchell from getting his way. But the press wouldn't let go of the idea, mainly because Mitchell stayed in the news by firing away at the entrenched thinking of the admirals.

Mitchell was confident that he would win out in the long run. As the Deputy Chief of the Air Service, he ordered planes, pilots and mechanics to Langley Field, Virginia, for bombing training. The main aircraft to be used were Martin bombers and DH-4s. Doolittle was assigned as an engineering officer and flight leader in one of the DH-4 squadrons.

Besides day bombing practice, Doolittle and other pilots were told to try bombing at night. Large fires were to be built along the beach of a deserted island to serve as targets.

On the first night of the experiment, Doolittle went aloft with three other planes in formation. Each plane had four 100-pound bombs under each wing. They climbed out from Langley and leveled off. Doolittle spotted a large fire below and ordered his flight into trail formation. He lined up on the flaming target and pulled the bomb release handle. The bombs plummeted downward and landed very close to the fire.

The next morning, Doolittle asked the sergeant in charge of setting the target fires, how close he and the other pilots had come with their bombs.

"Lieutenant, this may come as a shock to you, but we never did get out to that island last night because the boat engine wouldn't start. I don't know whose fire you bombed but it wasn't one we started!"

Jimmy was shocked. He waited and worried about the possible consequences of having bombed a fire of some beach camper. He waited in vain. No report was ever received that anyone's firesite had been bombed and no one was ever known to have been hurt. To this day, he has no idea who might have started that fire or exactly what it was that he bombed that night in 1921.

History has recorded that Billy Mitchell won his argument about the superiority of airplanes over battleships. The *Ostfriesland*, believed unsinkable, slid beneath the waves off the Virginia

coast as did the *Frankfurt,* another German battlewagon. Ironically, however, a board made up of army and navy officers later
wrote a report saying that nothing had been proven by the tests
and that the battleship was still "the backbone of the fleet."

Although Mitchell was later court-martialed for his airpower
preachings, Jimmy Doolittle had great respect for the principles
his fiery superior espoused. Although he agreed with Mitchell's
theories, he did not especially agree with the methods Mitchell
used to get them across to the American people. Several years
later, the controversial air general was reduced to the grade of
colonel and eventually resigned from the service.

Once back in San Antonio, Jimmy continued with his plan to
span the country in a modified DH-4. Encouraged by Mitchell,
who wanted his airmen to do anything within reason to keep
military airpower in the public eye, Jimmy worked day and
night stripping all the weight possible out of his plane and in-
stalling extra tanks. News of his planned attempt leaked out in
May 1922, when he made a nonstop flight from San Antonio to
San Diego in 12 hours and 30 minutes. Now certain that he could
set a new coast-to-coast record, Jimmy flew to Pablo Beach near
Jacksonville, Florida, where a number of newspaper reporters
were waiting to observe his takeoff.

The next morning, before dawn, Jimmy checked his airplane
over and was ready. A few reporters gathered along the beach
and Doolittle waved at them with all the confidence of a circus
acrobat about to perform a death-defying stunt before a rapt
audience. Pulling his goggles down over his eyes with a flourish,
Jimmy pushed the throttle forward and roared down the beach.
He gathered speed and the DH-4's tail lifted gently off the
ground. Suddenly, instead of rising off the sand, the plane slewed
toward the water, caught a wingtip in the surf, dove nose-first
under the waves, and ended up on its back.

The sudden stop and the rush of water all over his body
stunned Jimmy. He opened his safety belt, fell out on his head,
and for a moment thought he was going to drown. He thrashed
around wildly trying to extricate himself and thought sure that

he couldn't hold his breath long enough to escape. Just as he thought he was finished, his feet touched bottom and he stood up. The water was only two feet deep!

The cheers that had accompanied his takeoff quickly turned to laughter when the cocky but now soggy Doolittle plodded onto the beach. Jimmy vowed that from that moment on, he would not tell the press about any record attempts because there was always the risk of failure. Failure, he reasoned, was not only indicative of poor planning on his part but was bad publicity for the Air Service. This had been an avoidable accident. He had not counted on the possibility that soft sand spots could spoil the best-laid plans for a flight. Next time he would not be so cocky. And there would be no crowds there to laugh if he goofed again.

6. Coast-to-Coast in Less than a Day

FORTUNATELY, THE MODIFIED DH-4 was not so badly damaged that it couldn't be repaired. Doolittle made a full report of the mishap to his superiors and then requested permission to try again. To his surprise, his request was promptly approved. The DH-4 repairs were completed by September 1, and Jimmy returned to Pablo Beach—this time without the advance publicity he had on the first attempt.

At 6 P.M. on September 4, 1922, Jimmy said good-bye to some friends at Jacksonville and made the forty-minute hop to Pablo Beach. He was met there by a few mechanics who had set out a row of lanterns down the beach to mark a runway. Jimmy described the flight to Kelly Field, Texas, this way:

> I was determined to take no chances of failure on this second attempt. The row of lanterns helped me keep away from the surf yet stay on the hard beach area.
>
> I taxied down the beach at about 45 miles an hour and when I thought everything was all right I gave the Liberty engine full throttle. The tail came up nicely and I was airborne fairly quickly. Turning toward the Atlantic briefly, I banked westward and settled

49

down for the long flight to San Antonio which I thought would take about eleven hours.

A full moon greeted me for about two hours after the start. I was then flying at an altitude of 3,500 feet and at a speed of 105 miles an hour. A favoring wind was on my quarter. A severe thunder and lightning storm then came up. I realized it was too extensive in area to dodge, and plunged directly into it, trusting to my compass to steer a straight course. At each flash of lightning I peeked over the side of the cockpit, saw familiar landmarks and, after consulting my maps spread out before me, knew that I was flying high and free and true.

Over New Orleans the rain, sweeping in gusts, stung my face. This rain continued until after I had passed Iberia, on the Texas border. By veering a little to the northward I passed out of the storm area. From that time until I landed at Kelly Field, San Antonio, I encountered nothing but pleasant weather. It was a wonderful sight to see dawn breaking over the Texas country and to feel the thrill of having successfully completed half of my journey through the long hours of darkness. There is an exhilaration in night flying which more than makes up for the solitude and the incessant purr of the motor.

As has been typical of Jimmy Doolittle ever since the crowd laughed at him on his first attempt, he does not elaborate on his accomplishments. The *Air Corps Newsletter,* an official journal for army airmen, gave more details:

Long before daylight, people began to assemble at Kelly Field to watch for the arrival of the "Lone Pilot" who was to make a new record for American aviation. They came from all parts of the surrounding country and in all sorts of cars. . . .

As dawn broke and no sign appeared of Lieutenant Doolittle, his comrades began to be a bit anxious, and from time to time recalled the bad points along the route from New Orleans. Finally, this spirit could no longer be continued, and several ships took the air to look for him in the low clouds. Among the hundreds present, all the aviation activities in the district were represented—from the Air Office, Eighth Corps Area, to his brother officers from neighboring fields. Finally, after two or three false alarms as ships that took the air to look for him returned, a lone ship glided into the field at 7:05 A.M., September 5, and a cheer went up that proclaimed to the world that the first leg of the greatest transcontinetal "one-man trip" had been accomplished. As soon as the motor was cut a picked outfit of enlisted men hopped to work, and while Lieutenant Doolittle was getting a much-needed breakfast and a chance to stretch his legs, they gassed, oiled, and watered the plane. The ship was completely gone over, wires tightened, radiator leak repaired, motor examined, and when the Lieutenant took the stick 1 hour and 15 minutes later everything was in order.

At 8:20 A.M., September 5, the great ship once again took the air and slowly climbed toward the low ceiling. Everyone was now confident that the trip would be made; for, in spite of the bad weather, Doolittle would be flying over country with which he was well acquainted, due to his border service, and would have daylight to help him in reading his maps. He was accompanied on his trip by planes from the field as far as Medina Lake, although one went along as far as El Paso.

The last leg of the flight had concerned Jimmy—not because he feared he would get lost, but because he thought the drone of the Liberty engine and fatigue would make him dangerously sleepy. A few days before he had left San Antonio with the repaired plane, he had written a letter to his friend, Lt. John McCulloch, then adjutant at Rockwell Field, and asked:

> Please send two pace-making planes to meet me either at El Centro, California, or Yuma, Arizona. This will give me something to think about and help keep me awake. You see, I will have been in the air from 20 to 25 hours with only one 30-minute stop at Kelly for gas and oil, so I will be pretty tired.

When the word had been flashed to San Diego that Doolittle was on his way past El Paso, Capt. William Randolph and Lt. C. L. Webber were sent aloft to intercept him.

Randolph and Webber arrived over Yuma and began circling. Just when it seemed they would have to turn back to refuel, Doolittle's DH-4 appeared out of the east. Groggy from wrestling the plane over the mountains, the sight of his two buddies snapped him awake. He signalled for them to get in formation on each wing and the three planes raced to Rockwell and landed. Actual flying time, coast-to-coast 21 hours, 19 minutes—a record and the first time anyone had crossed the continent by air in less than a day!

Jimmy could not linger in San Diego. The *Air Corps Newsletter* explains why:

Although extensive plans had been made for his reception at San Diego, it was impossible to carry out same, due to orders he received from the War Department to report for duty at McCook Field. He only remained in the California city long enough to rest up, and on Friday at 8:00 A.M., September 8, he once more took off for Kelly Field, arriving at 7:40 P.M.

While he tried to surprise them at Kelly Field by gliding in at dusk, word of his departure had been received, and he found the Comanding Officer at Kelly Field waiting for him at the head of the reception committee. As soon as he cut his motor he was bundled into a car with his proud wife and mother, and was conducted at the head of all the private automobiles at Kelly Field to the City Hall, where the Mayor and members of the city government and various civic organizations were waiting to present him the "freedom of the city" and show him what San Antonio thought of his feat. After a short address by the Mayor and Colonel Howard, and a reply by Lieutenant Doolittle, the tired aviator was escorted to an awaiting automobile, and with the Kelly Field band at the head, followed by a fleet of automobiles, paraded through the principal streets of San Antonio.

It was expected that Lieutenant Doolittle would remain in San Antonio for several days to close up his business affairs, but he quietly slipped away the morning of September 9 for his new station at McCook Field, not so quietly, however, but that his old squadron, the 90th, was able to learn of it and give him an escort far beyond the limits of San Antonio. . . .

This great flight merely served to emphasize the possibilities of the airplane and what hopes the future holds out for commercial lines. . . . Jimmy Doolittle had indeed struck a spark of hope in young airmen's breasts the nation over.

Although the record was recognized as official and Doolittle received much publicity because of his feat, apparently the War Department did not feel at the time that any more of a reward was necessary or deserved. Seven years later, however, spurred by some anonymous person somewhere in government, a citation was belatedly drawn up for the award of the Distinguished Flying Cross. It said:

> For extraordinary achievement while participating in an aerial flight. On September 4-5, 1922, Lieutenant Doolittle accomplished a one-stop flight from Pablo Beach, Florida, to San Diego, California, in 22 hours and 30 minutes elapsed time, an extraordinary achievement with the equipment available at that time. By his skill, endurance, and resourcefulness he demonstrated the possibility of moving Air Corps units to any portion of the United States in less than 24 hours, thus reflecting great credit on himself and the Army of the United States.

The coast-to-coast flight of 1922 marked the beginning of many distance and speed record attempts by army aviators. Lts. Oakley J. Kelly and John A. Macready tried to fly nonstop across the country in a Fokker T-2 aircraft. They failed twice, then decided to try for an endurance record. They succeeded by remaining in the air more than thirty-six hours, which proved to them that the airplane and its engine could endure sustained flight for such a long period. They then tried again for the nonstop coast-to-coast "first" and finally succeeded on May 2, 1923, by flying the 2,516 miles in 26 hours and 50 minutes. Although they did not beat Jimmy's record, they made the trip without refueling—the farthest any plane had yet been flown.

Meanwhile, Jimmy had settled down at McCook Field near Dayton, Ohio, with his now-growing family to which two boys had been added—Jimmy, Jr., and John. He became deeply involved in the engineering work at McCook, which was the major research and testing center for the nation's air force. In the aftermath of World War I and under the stimulus of Billy Mitchell's prodding to develop an air force equal to or better than that of any other nation, there were thousands of questions about flight that had to be answered. The men assigned to research had to deal continually with the unknowns of flying. They had to explore and push back the frontiers of man's knowledge. In short, they were pioneers who risked their reputations and their lives to answer the basic questions of designing planes that were safe and reliable and of solving the mysteries of what men had to do to fly them ever faster, higher, and farther.

It was into this atmosphere of aeronautical research that Doolittle was thrust. His successful record flight and past work as an engineering officer had made him a likely candidate to help explore the expanding dimension of the airman. Furthermore, he was now a college graduate because the University of California had conferred the Bachelor of Arts degree on him a few weeks after his gallant flight, giving him full credit for the final semester he had not completed when he had joined the Air Service five years before.

In addition to taking part in actual flight tests during the next eight months, Jimmy attended the Air Corps Engineering School at McCook and developed a keen appreciation for the work of test pilots and the knowledge they needed to do their jobs. He studied hard and decided that his future lay in the science of aeronautics. Although the Engineering School was good, he felt that concentrated work at an academic institution would be better. Consequently, he applied for entrance to the Massachusetts Institute of Technology to work toward a Master of Science degree. He was promptly accepted and in July 1923 moved Jo and the boys to Boston for two years of tough but rewarding engineering courses.

If you ask Jimmy Doolittle about those two years, he says that he couldn't have passed the grueling MIT courses without his wife's help. She typed his notes and term papers, listened to his discussions of engineering problems, helped express his thoughts in plain terms, and worried with him about examinations.

"There's no doubt about it," he says. "I would have flunked out if it hadn't been for Jo. I was not a brilliant student and I think I passed some of my courses only because of the beautiful typing job she did on my term papers."

Of course, no one has ever gone through MIT solely on the basis of good typing. Jimmy's intense scientific curiosity, persistence, and spirit of competition also helped. He was determined not to muff the excellent educational opportunity the army had given him. He passed all courses, received his master's degree in 1924 and promptly asked to remain to continue work toward a doctorate. Again he was accepted and continued the tough grind. It would normally have been a two-year stint but Jimmy decided he must do it in a single year. He took more than the normal number of courses and crammed long and hard to meet all the degree requirements.

Just as Jimmy was within sight of his goal, he received orders in March 1924 to return to McCook Field to conduct important tests on pursuit aircraft. His job was to fly the planes to the limits of their design and determine just how strong planes should be made to withstand the rigors of air combat. To put it simply, he was supposed to dive the planes at maximum power, pull out, and see how much they could stand. He was to see how much it would take to pull the wings off and strain the fuselages to the breaking point in order to verify the engineering data that had been accumulated from wind tunnel and stress tests conducted while the planes were on the ground.

The job was ideal for Jimmy. He was now one of those rare individuals who could speak aeronautical engineering language on the ground and apply it in the air. When he returned to earth, he could now report on the plane's performance in engineering terms instead of in the imprecise terms of a pilot who had no engineering education.

Although Jimmy was at McCook for only a brief period, his experiments and the results he obtained were priceless in terms of what he accomplished at this critical period in American aviation, which has been called "the trial-and-error days." For this work of about three weeks, Jimmy received reward in the form of a second Distinguished Flying Cross. Like the first one, it was not awarded until 1929—five years after he had earned it. The citation explains in succinct terms what he accomplished:

During March, 1924, at McCook Field, Dayton, Ohio, Lieutenant Doolittle, piloting a Fokker PW-7 pursuit airplane performed a series of acceleration tests requiring skill, initiative, endurance, and courage of the highest type. In these tests a recording accelerometer was mounted in the airplane and the accelerations taken for the following maneuvers: loops at various air speeds, single and multiple barrel rolls, power spirals, tail spins, power on and power off, half loop, half roll, and Immelmann turn; inverted flight; pulling out of dive at various air speeds; flying the airplane on a level course with considerable angle of bank; and flying in bumpy air. In these tests the airplane was put through the most extreme maneuvers possible in order that the flight loads imposed upon the wings of the airplane under extreme conditions of air combat might be ascertained. These tests were put through with that fine combination of fearlessness and skill which constitutes the essence of distinguished flying. Through them scientific data of great and permanent importance to the Air Corps were obtained.

Jimmy returned to MIT to continue his studies and to decide upon a thesis topic for his doctoral degree. Thinking back on his flying career thus far, he recalled his record-setting cross-country flight of 1922 and concluded that if aircraft were ever to become a safe and reliable means of transportation, one basic problem had to be solved: the airplane had to be able to take off, fly, and land in all kinds of weather. This meant that pilots had to be able to fly in clouds, without seeing outside the cockpit. Hundreds of pilots had gone to their deaths because of bad weather—the bugaboo of aviation that had to be licked.

Aviation, in the 1920s, was emerging into a bold new age and had come through some elementary steps in regard to weather flying in arriving at this point. In the early days of flying, a slight breeze could delay or cancel a flight. It was customary for a pilot to wet his finger and hold it up. If there was enough air movement to cause uneven evaporation and make one side cooler than the other, there was too much wind to fly.

When the planes were stronger, a good breeze was welcomed because it shortened landing and takeoff distances. Then came the period when a pilot was concerned only when he couldn't see the visible horizon. He would fly through clouds briefly but he wanted to come out the other side into clear air and be able to find the horizon when he emerged. It was found that no pilot could fly for long in clouds without losing his sense of balance. He suffered vertigo and became dizzy. Sooner or later, he would be completely disoriented and put his plane into a stall, spin, or dive. Many pilots were killed during the '20s and '30s because they were unable to figure out which side was up before they crashed.

Jimmy had been aware of this phenomenon. In his record-setting flight across the United States, he had installed an experimental bank-and-turn indicator—a new instrument that had been invented in 1917 by Elmer Sperry, Sr. Jimmy Doolittle describes the 1922 flight and why he took an interest in instrument flying:

I took off just after dark from Pablo Beach. I had chosen a moonlight night to facilitate night navigation but about four hours out, I ran into solid overcast and then severe thunderstorms.

For a while, lightning flashes were almost constant and, in the otherwise black night, so intense as to clearly light up the ground for a considerable area. Some flashes were so close that their familiar ozone odor could be detected. Although it seemed that one could reach out and touch them, none struck the plane.

The air was extremely turbulent and the airplane was violently thrown about its axes as well as up and down. Although the DH-4 had excellent stability characteristics, I could hold it on a relatively even keel only with great concentration and effort. After the lightning died away, the turbulence appeared to intensify and there was about an hour in the jet black darkness when no ground reference point could be seen and it would have been quite impossible to maintain proper altitude and course without that bank-and-turn indicator.

Although I had been flying for almost five years "by the seat of my pants" and considered that I'd achieved some skill at it, this particular flight made me a firm believer in proper instrumentation for bad weather flying.

The requirement to do some original research into some aspect of flying for his doctoral program gave Jimmy the opportunity to explore further the effects of wind on airplane performance. The thesis was entitled, "The Effect of the Wind Velocity Gradient," and its author employed wind tunnel data, flight tests, and mathematical analysis. It starts out:

There has long been an uncertainty in the minds of aviators regarding the effect of the wind on the flying qualities of an airplane.

Some pilots claim that it is much easier to turn into the wind than with it, and that at any altitude they can tell the wind direction by the feel of the ship in a turn and this even though in a dense cloud which would preclude the possibility of obtaining their relative motion from any stationary object.

Other pilots maintain that, regardless of the wind velocity or the proximity of the ground, there is no difference in the feel of the plane when turning into the wind and when turning with it. They claim that any apparent difference is due wholly to the psychological effect on the pilot, resulting from the difference in ground speed in the two cases. If there is any difference in the ship's performance, from a time-altitude standpoint, it is because the pilot handled the controls differently. In other words, if the pilot were blindfolded he could not tell the wind direction when turning and a turn made into the wind would be identical with a turn made with the wind. This is, of course, considering the turn in relation to the medium in which it is being executed and not in relation to the curves traced out on the ground.

There is a similar difference of opinion regarding the effect of a strong wind on the rate of climb. Experienced pilots are about evenly divided, half feeling that a plane climbs better into the wind, and the other half feeling that the wind makes absolutely no difference.

From his study and calculations, Doolittle concluded that: (1) There is no measurable effect in level flight, at altitude, due to wind direction as long as the wind is steady; (2) there is no effect on climb due to wind except very near the ground and there the wind velocity gradient increases the rate of climb slightly when flying into the wind and decreases it slightly when flying with the wind; (3) a steady wind has no effect on turning except very near the ground when the wind velocity gradient causes a slight tendency to settle when turning away from a head wind and a slight tendency to climb when turning into it. This is most noticeable in strong winds and when flying at a large angle of attack or at minimum power.

He summed up his research this way:

A steady wind exercises no measurable effect on airplane performance at altitude except, of course, on speed and direction of flight. Very near the ground, however, the effect of wind velocity gradient can be serious, particularly in the case of a heavily loaded airplane. The danger is increased by a strong tendency on the part of the pilot to pull the nose up or in beyond the most efficient angle of attack. This increases any tendency to settle and may even cause the airplane to stall and spin in.

Although these conclusions may seem primitive in light of to-day's knowledge of aeronautics, they provided one of the first scientific inquiries into a vital aspect of weather flying—the effects of wind on an aircraft in flight.

Jimmy was rewarded for his two years of hard work when he was awarded the Doctor of Science in Aeronautics degree in 1925—one of the first ever to be granted in the United States.

7. The Crazy Yankee

His college work now completed at age 28, Jimmy's orders returned him to the Army's Engineering Depot at McCook Field. As soon as he settled his wife and two boys into their quarters, he was back in the cockpit continuing to test the army's newest planes. By this time, he had become well known throughout the army's air arm and the press was intrigued by the fact that a daring pilot could achieve the highest degree in engineering.

But Jimmy was not about to believe that he had achieved all he was capable of. What he had done thus far was only a beginning. He intended to use his engineering knowledge to the utmost for the improvement of planes and the safety of pilots.

After only two months on the job at McCook, Jimmy was given instructions to report for temporary duty at the Anacostia Naval Air Station in Washington, D.C. Now a recognized speed and stunt flier, he was being given the opportunity to learn to fly seaplanes. Although by now he had flown almost every fast land-plane in flight tests at McCook, he had very little experience flying from the water. The only difference in the planes is that pontoons replace the wheels, but water takeoffs and landings are different from those of grass or hard-surfaced runways. Generally, more distance is needed for a takeoff run and a pilot must learn to break the surface tension of the water before he can lift off. He must appreciate the dangers inherent in landing and taking off when waves can cause a pontoon or wing float to dig in and capsize a plane. And he must learn to taxi on the water without brakes and to dock a plane without smashing into a pier.

There was a cogent reason for sending Doolittle to the Navy for seaplane training. Billy Mitchell, by now an outspoken critic of those who could not understand the future of airpower as he saw it, was about to be court-martialed for his views. Mitchell wanted a separate air force equal to the army and navy and had gone too far in his criticism of those who opposed his ideas. What was needed was proof that the army's planes were inadequate and obsolete so that the public would bring pressure on Congress to appropriate more funds for land-based aviation.

In order to focus attention on military aviation, an air show was planned to be held at Mitchel Field, Long Island, in October 1925. In addition to acrobatics, parachute jumps, mock aerial combat, and other stunts to thrill the large crowds expected, an attempt would be made at a world speed record for landplanes in the race for the Pulitzer Trophy. Later that month, American pilots would try to capture the Schneider Cup and establish a world seaplane record.

As part of the master scheme, the army and navy had agreed to split the cost of a racing plane. For $500,000, four Curtiss R3Cs were purchased, along with newly designed Curtiss V-1400 (620 hp) engines. One plane was static-tested to a "near-destruction" stage, leaving three for record attempts. The R3Cs were designed to be flown with either wheels or pontoons.

Lt. (jg.) Alford Williams was chosen as the acceptance test pilot for the navy and Cyrus Bettis and Doolittle were the army pilots. For the Pulitzer Race, it was decided by the flip of a coin that Bettis would be the army entry, leaving Doolittle as his alternate. If Doolittle did not compete against Williams, he would be the army entry for the Schneider Cup.

While Bettis prepared the army R3C, Doolittle was scheduled

to put on an acrobatic show to give the crowd a preliminary thrill. He did. Climbing to altitude in a Curtiss pursuit plane while an announcer set the stage, Jimmy decided to do his bit to attract public attention to military airpower. For the next half hour, he performed every maneuver in the book: loops, chandelles, Immelmanns, Cuban 8s, lazy 8s, slow rolls, and power dives down to within a few hundred feet over the crowd. He saved his best stunt until last: inverted flight across the field just a few feet above the ground—a maneuver rarely done up to that time because engines ceased operating when inverted and there was no room for error on the part of the pilot.

The crowd gasped as Jimmy started a power dive at the field, leveled off, and slowly rolled over on his back. Then, for what seemed an eternity to the spectators, he zoomed across the field upside down and made an inverted climb until his speed gave out. At the crucial moment, he rolled right side up, did a wingover, and came roaring back at the crowd with throttle wide open. At that moment, some balloons were released and Jimmy zoomed up after them. One by one, he speared them with his propeller or wingtips until they were all gone.

Before the highly publicized Pulitzer Trophy Race was to be run, a preliminary race for the Billy Mitchell Trophy was scheduled. Ten pilots of the First Pursuit Group competed with PW-8 aircraft over a twelve-mile course. The winner was Lt. Thomas K. Mathews, who averaged a speed of 161.7 mph—typical speed for the pursuit planes then in the army inventory.

It was a cold and gusty afternoon, October 25, 1925, when the Pulitzer Race began. In addition to the R3C-1 racers flown by Williams and Bettis in the first heat, two navy fliers in older Curtiss pursuits, a PW-8, and a P-1 flown by army pilots were entered in the second heat. The race was for four laps over a 31.07-mile course.

Williams won the coin toss and was first off the ground. Two minutes later, Bettis shot off the blocks and began his race against the clock. Williams completed his first lap at better than his old mark of 243 mph over a closed course. The navy officials in the stands cheered when the time was announced. But Bettis

Doolittle had only a few flights in a pontoon-equipped plane before he won the Schneider Cup Race in 1925 in this Curtiss R3C-2. This aircraft can be seen at the Air Force Museum, Wright-Patterson Air Force Base, Ohio. (*Photo courtesy of the U.S. Air Force*)

Army and navy pilots before the Schneider Cup Race at Baltimore, Maryland, October 26, 1925. Left to right: Lt. George T. Cuddihy, USN; Lt. J. H. Doolittle, USA; Lt. Cyrus Bettis, USA; and Lt. Ralph Ofstie, USN. (*Photo courtesy of the U.S. Air Force*)

came streaking by in almost the identical time and the army rooters cheered lustily.

Williams could not equal his first lap time because of engine trouble, but Bettis upped his speed to 248 mph and then 249 mph over the final two laps for an average speed of 248.99 mph—a world's record for this type of course.

In the second heat, Army Lt. L. H. Dawson won the honors with a speed of 169.9 mph in his P-1, making it a great day for the army.

Watching all this on the ground, Doolittle was thoughtful. It was customary for the pilots to approach a pylon at a low altitude, kick their planes into a gut-wrenching turn, and then proceed to the next pylon. Since speed and lift are always lost when an airplane turns, he reasoned, wouldn't it be safer and faster if a pilot approached the pylon with a little more altitude and then dove as he rounded it? He decided to try it when he competed for the Schneider Cup.

The entry of the army into the Schneider Trophy Race was a U.S. "first." The first Schneider Trophy contest had been held in 1913 and only two countries—France and the United States—competed. The year 1925 was to be the ninth time that the race had been held. The United States had won it only once before—in 1923, when navy Lt. David Rittenhouse bested French and British entries with a speed of 177.38 mph in a Curtiss CR-3 seaplane.

Several days before the race was scheduled, Doolittle and the other pilots tuned their engines and made test flights in Baltimore Harbor, where the race was to be held. Lts. Ralph Ofstie and George Cuddihy were to fly two of the R3Cs and Doolittle the third. British pilots were slated to fly two Gloster-Napier racers and a Supermarine S-4, one of the sleekest planes ever built. Italian pilots brought two awkward-looking Macchi M-33 flying boats that seemed hopelessly outclassed.

Unfortunately for the British, the S-4 and one of the Glosters were wrecked on trial flights. When race time came, there were only six planes left.

Doolittle was first off the water and the other competitors

followed at the five-minute intervals specified in the rules. Within minutes after takeoff, both of the navy planes dropped out because of engine trouble. This left Doolittle, the single Gloster, and the two ungainly Macchis. It was an unfair race. Using his newly-discovered technique of diving at the pylons anchored in the river, Doolittle set new speed records on practically every lap. When the timers compared their watches, Doolittle was officially clocked at 232.573 mph—a new record for seaplanes over a closed course. Not satisfied, he took off again the next day and set still another record by averaging 245.713 mph for seaplanes over a three-kilometer straight course on three passes.

Again, fame had come to Doolittle and the headlines screeched not only that the United States had won the coveted Schneider Trophy but that it had been won by an army man who had very little experience in seaplanes. On October 14, 1925, *The New York Times* editorialized:

> . . . it must have been a grievous sight to sailors when Lieutenant James H. Doolittle, U.S.A., putting pontoons on his landplane, romped away with the cup which Lieutenant David Rittenhouse of the Navy brought over from England two years ago. But that was not the worst of it. The naval lieutenants Cuddihy and Ofstie had engine trouble, dropped out of the race and were "towed to safety." The Army men never seem to take tows in Neptune's realm.

When Jimmy returned to Dayton, he was given a surprise reception. His army buddies conferred upon him the title of honorary Navy Admiral. He and Jo were given a big dinner in downtown Dayton and were driven around the city in an automobile decorated like a ship. On its sides were signs proclaiming welcome to "Admiral James H. Doolittle."

The day that Doolittle won the Schneider Cup, it was announced that General William Mitchell would face a court-martial for his fiery speeches and writings about the poor state of American military aviation. Having reverted to his permanent grade of colonel from brigadier general, Mitchell had been re-

lieved of his job as deputy chief of the Air Service and sent to
Fort Sam Houston, Texas. From there, he continued to condemn
those who did not concur in his views about the necessity for a
strong and separate air force. On September 5, 1925, he handed
the press a nine-page statement that blasted "the incompetency,
criminal negligence, and almost treasonable administration of the
National Defense by the Navy and War Departments."

What had caused Mitchell to make such a statement were two
naval aviation disasters that had occurred in close succession
two weeks earlier. One had been the disappearance of a PN-9
plane trying to complete the first flight from the mainland to
Hawaii. The other had been the disastrous crash of the dirigible
Shenandoah after running into bad weather over Ohio.

The court-martial was called by President Calvin Coolidge to
determine whether or not Mitchell was guilty of conduct preju-
dicial to "good order and military discipline [and] . . . conduct
of a nature to bring discredit upon the military service." The
court declared him guilty on December 17, 1925.

Most army fliers felt in their hearts that the former number
two man in their branch of the service was right in pleading for a
stronger air force, but few agreed that any officer should go so
far as to accuse his superiors of "incompetency, criminal negligence, and almost treasonable administration." They knew that
Mitchell had decided to become a martyr for airpower and give
up his career for the cause. Although the court did not take away
his commission, he was sentenced to five years suspension from
active duty without pay or allowances. However, President Coolidge changed the sentence to five years suspension at half pay.
Rather than accept this fate, Mitchell elected to resign and gave
up all claims to any retirement benefits.

Doolittle, as a first lieutenant, could do nothing to influence
the outcome. Instead of lamenting how poor American military
aviation was, he decided he would rather use his talents and
skills to improve it. Winning the Schneider Cup Race brought
him national acclaim for performance instead of theories. He
preferred it that way.

After the publicity of the Schneider Race had subsided, Jimmy was made chief of the Test Flight Section at Wright Field, the successor to the older McCook Field. His job was to supervise all assigned test pilots and be in charge of all experimental flying—a job he considered the best in the army. As top man, he could pick and choose the tests he wanted to conduct personally and his engineering background gave him the knowledge he needed to determine which tests might make the most significant contribution to aviation.

One story is typical of this period in his life. It concerns the concept of a rudder trim tab which someone had conceived on paper but had not proven in flight. Instead of a piece of metal being attached to a rudder to correct for any tendency of a plane to stray off course, the new tab was installed as part of the rudder and could be adjusted inside the cockpit. Would it give a pilot the needed advantage or would it tear the rudder off if moved to extreme positions? Doolittle chose to find out for himself.

He took off with a fellow pilot, Lt. James E. Hutchison, and climbed to the test area. Doolittle then proceeded to put the plane through a series of stalls, rolls, spins, and loops, each time placing the trim tab in a different position. At the extreme setting on the tab, a severe shudder developed and before Jimmy could reduce it, the rudder control wires broke.

Hutchison, in the rear seat, sat wide-eyed and wondered what was going to happen next. Doolittle, using the ailerons, quickly leveled off and looked back at his passenger.

"You all right?" he yelled above the engine noise.

Hutchison nodded.

"Want to bail out?" Doolittle shouted.

"Not if you don't," Hutchison replied.

"I think we can get her down O.K.," Doolittle said.

Hutchison replied by giving his boss the familiar thumb and forefinger circle sign and grinned.

Nursing the plane down from altitude with ailerons alone, Jimmy slipped over the end of the Wright Field runway to a smooth landing and taxied to the parking area. As far as he was concerned, the new trim tab did not work and needed more engineering to prevent a recurrence. To the young test pilots standing around and staring in disbelief at the tail of the airplane, their boss had just proven something that had been argued about for years. It *was* possible to land an airplane without rudder control. Another aviation myth had just been shattered.

While Jimmy was devoting his time to such tests, his name was being mentioned in Washington, D.C., and New York. It was now 1926 and the Air Service had its name changed to Army Air Corps but that didn't mean that government appropriations were forthcoming to develop the kind of planes the army needed. What was needed to keep the aircraft industry alive and enable it to conduct the kind of research necessary to make the United States a first-rate air power was a market for planes. Top executives of the Curtiss airplane firm went to Washington and asked the War Department to lend them a pilot to demonstrate their new P-1 fighter in South America.

"And who is the pilot you want, as if we didn't know?" War Department officials asked. "Doolittle?"

The Curtiss officials nodded. Doolittle's engineering degrees and his reputation as a stunt pilot, test pilot, and trophy-winning racing pilot made him the best possible airplane salesman.

Permission was granted because the Air Corps had much to gain from cooperation with the aircraft industry. Doolittle was given a leave of absence without pay and went by ship to Santiago, Chile, along with the Curtiss P-1 and a mechanic, Boyd Sherman.

Jimmy didn't know what to expect upon arrival. As a flying salesman of a single-seat pursuit plane, he imagined that he was to put on a one-man air show for Chilean government officials. He found, however, that he was only one of a number of plane salesmen there. German, French, Italian, and British manufacturers had sent their best machines and pilots for the same reason. The Chileans wanted them to compete against each other so that they could choose the best aircraft for their budding air force.

This was to Doolittle's liking. It was a competition where one man matched his skill and judgment against others in the air. He was delighted.

Before the scheduled competition, a big cocktail party was to be held for the foreign guest pilots in an officer's club. There are many versions of what happened that night but it is said that Jimmy Doolittle was introduced to a drink called the "pisco sour," a specialty of the fun-loving Chileans. During the course of the evening the subject of Douglas Fairbanks, the famous acrobatic actor of silent films, came up. His legendary balcony-leaping, sword-playing roles had captured the imaginations of the romantic Latins in the motion pictures that were then playing to crowded audiences all over South America.

Although Jimmy was not conversant in Spanish, he sensed the admiration that his hosts had for the handsome American actor. For some devilish reason he cannot explain himself, he interjected a comment that "Doug Fairbanks is not especially talented as an acrobat. All American kids can do those things."

When the remark was translated into Spanish, it was interpreted as an outlandish statement that needed some proving. From the dubious looks and raised eyebrows of the other pilots, there was nothing left for Doolittle to do but prove that *he* could tumble, leap, and do one-hand stands as easily as Fairbanks. He handed his drink to a friend, wheeled up on end into a handstand and then began walking on his hands through the crowded club lounge. When he regained his feet, there was polite clapping but it wasn't enough to satisfy the acrobat-turned-pilot. He moved over to a window, went out to a balcony and threw himself into a handstand on the railing, which happened to be one story above a courtyard below. Again there was applause, but Doolittle wasn't through yet. There was a narrow stone ledge below a window. He climbed out of the window and then, grasping the ledge with one hand, he extended his body straight out parallel with the ground—a feat requiring strong arms and a knowledge of body leverage.

There were shouts of "Bravo!" and "Olé!" as the daring American seemed suspended in space. But Doolittle could feel something slip beneath the arm that was curled over the ledge. To his dismay, the ledge slowly tore loose and he plunged to the courtyard below with the stone ledge shattered all around him.

It took a while to get the dazed Doolittle to the hospital but when he did, X rays showed that the daring American had broken both ankles. Now he would be unable to demonstrate his plane at the trials two days hence.

Doolittle was furious with himself for attempting such a trick. He wouldn't do anything foolish in an airplane without first testing the machine's limitations as well as his own.

As the doctors put casts on both legs, they told him he would have to remain in bed for several weeks and that he would have to wear the casts for about two months. Doolittle's anger grew. When the story got back to the States, he knew he would be the laughingstock of the Air Corps. Worse yet, the Curtiss company would have no orders and the foreigners would have gotten all the glory for their planes. The German ace, Ernst von Schonabeck, was scheduled to show off a new Dornier which many believed to be the best of the foreign planes there. Doolittle knew the Curtiss P-1 was better but now he couldn't prove it.

The thought of failure on his mission was too much for Doolittle. He sent for Boyd Sherman.

"I'm going to fly that airplane, Boyd," he said in his hospital bed through gritted teeth. "You make me some clips so my feet won't slip off the rudder pedals and have that plane ready to go for me when the demonstrations start."

Sherman nodded and went to work. Two days later, while the President of Chile, who had sent expressions of sympathy to the bedridden American, looked on, an ambulance pulled up beside the P-1 that Sherman had been warming up. Doolittle was helped out of the ambulance into the cockpit, where Sherman had fixed the clips to each cast.

At that moment, von Schonabeck, an arrogant boaster, was putting the Dornier through a solo acrobatic routine that caused the Chileans to applaud time and time again.

"Get the chocks out, Boyd!" Doolittle shouted. "What that guy needs is some competition!"

Doolittle roared off the ground with the Curtiss-Wright engine wide open. Climbing to the altitude of the German, Jimmy roared by him in a pursuit pass and the World War I ace immediately sensed the challenge. He zoomed after the diving Curtiss, only to find that the Dornier was badly outclassed. The sensitive P-1 could be whipped into reverse turns and climb so fast that the Dornier seemed clumsy by comparison. The German pilot was continually embarrassed to find the American plane on his tail and then flash by him so that the Dornier would be rocked by the P-1's prop wash.

The German pilot suddenly broke off the engagement and headed for the airport. As he did, Doolittle noticed that a huge piece of fabric had torn loose from the Dornier's upper wing, certainly not a good sign for a plane that was supposed to withstand the rigors of combat.

Doolittle circled as the German landed and then roared across the field in a victory pass—inverted. The crowd cheered madly. Never before had they seen such flying. The American had not only beaten the German but had done it with both legs in casts! What better proof than that was needed to know which plane was superior?

The flight had not been easy for Doolittle. The scrappy fighter plane demanded pressure on those rudder pedals and pressure meant pain. When he landed, the pain almost made him pass out but he quickly revived when he received the rousing welcome from the crowd.

The casts on both legs were now strained and cracked from the exertion and needed to be replaced. But the Chilean doctor refused to have anything to do with the crazy Yankee. Doolittle, intent upon keeping the schedule that the Curtiss people had set, got Boyd Sherman to find an artificial limb maker who made him two strong, reinforced casts. When the time came for the trip to Bolivia, the next stop, Doolittle had his feet fitted into the clips and took off for La Paz, the two-mile high capital with the highest airport in the world (13,000 feet).

The reception Doolittle received in Bolivia was less than cordial. The landlocked, tin-rich country had long been fearful of

Chile and was suspicious of anyone flying a warplane from there. Shortly after his arrival, a mob gathered outside the Strangers Club where Doolittle was staying and began shouting anti-American slogans. Army troops were called to disperse the crowd but the Bolivian officials had gotten the message. Although Doolittle did demonstrate the plane the next day, there was no official indication of interest. The Bolivians did not want to buy the same type of plane that the Chileans were going to buy. Jimmy returned to Santiago puzzled by the Latin rationale.

The next stop was Buenos Aires, Argentina. It meant flying across the Andes Mountains, the treacherous mountain chain that runs the length of South America. It was a hazardous flight at that time but was more so for Doolittle. Not only was he flying a single-engine plane with both legs in casts, but he had to do it without a parachute since he could not unclip his feet to bail out if his engine failed.

The risk was a challenge to Doolittle. He made the trip and chalked up a South American aviation "first" for himself. He was the first American to fly across the Andes. Few people ever knew how much of a risk it really was.

The Argentinians bought the P-1 for its air force and Doolittle sailed home in the summer of 1926, his legs still in casts. Ahead of him were many weeks in Walter Reed Hospital so that his mangled ankles could heal properly.

8. The End of Seat-of-the-Pants Flying

THE ARMY DOCTORS GAVE Doolittle an order: stay in bed for six months. To a man who had never had an extended illness in his life and was as physically vigorous as Doolittle, it was like a prison sentence. With ankles immobilized and his body totally inactive, he was sure he could never last out six months flat on his back.

The six months of recuperation did not slow down his mind, however. It gave him a chance to recall his flying experiences and think about what he would do when he got back in the cockpit. He thought of new acrobatic stunts that had never been attempted and recalled one that all pilots thought impossible—an outside loop.

The normal, or inside, loop is a relatively easy maneuver in any airplane. Nose the plane down to gather some speed, pull back firmly but steadily on the stick until the plane is inverted on top. Then maintain enough pressure to pull the plane through and back into level flight. The only difficulty is experienced if not enough speed is obtained at the start or if the pilot exerts too much control pressure and the plane stalls and falls into a spin. The only physical sensation is that of the extra "G-force," which

73

pins a pilot into his seat, and a possible blackout when blood is forced out of his head toward his feet.

In an outside loop, the pilot would be on the outside of the circle and tremendous forces would be acting on his body as well as on the plane. If a plane was strong enough to withstand the maneuver, could a man's head take the centrifugal force that would tend to burst his blood vessels and force his vital organs toward his throat?

After much paper figuring and analysis of the stresses that would be placed on an aircraft in an outside loop, Doolittle concluded that the average fighter plane, stressed to withstand about seven times the force of gravity, could take the strain. What he could not calculate was the effect on a man. When he asked the doctors, all they could do was shrug their shoulders. To their knowledge, no one had ever tried to find out; besides, why would anyone want to try something like that?

The question became an obsession and when Jimmy's ankles healed, he went back to his job at Dayton, determined to find the answer. Anxious to get back to test flying, he was soon back in the cockpit of the Curtiss pursuit plane and practicing acrobatics. When he felt sure that his reactions were back to the sharpness he had known on the South American tour, he began a series of maneuvers which would lead to the eventual try at making an outside loop. He flew inverted for extended periods and then practiced pushing the nose up into an upside down climb until the speed was gone. He would analyze his own reactions, then return to earth to check the plane over. Back in the air again, he would go a step further and try diving and then pushing over into inverted flight. Again, there was the self-analysis and a check of the plane on the ground. Just as he thought—the sturdy pursuit plane took the strain. Since he had no lasting reactions other than the temporary discomfort of having "redouts" because of the blood rushing to his head, he kept going a step further each flight. Finally, on May 25, 1927, he decided to make the try. He told a few of his fellow pilots what he planned to do and then took off.

Word spread quickly down the flying line and pilots, mechanics, and technicians watched him climb the Curtiss into the clear air over the field. Doolittle leveled off at 10,000 feet and checked his seat belt and shoulder harness. Satisfied, he gave the little plane full throttle and nosed over into a power dive. The altimeter began to unwind as the airspeed indicator flicked toward the red mark of 350 miles per hour—the design limit of the plane. At this point, Doolittle pushed the nose under and, with the help of the elevator trim tab, was soon inverted. Now each second spent inverted meant a loss of speed so, fighting the tremendous pressure of blood forced into his head and the inevitable red-out, he continued to push forward on the nose so that it once again reached for the sky. Speed was rapidly diminishing now and Doolittle continued the pressure before he became unconscious. Just as he thought he had failed, the nose swung over the top and dropped underneath the horizon. He had completed an outside loop!

As before, Jimmy analyzed his reactions and found that his head was clear a few seconds after the centrifugal pressure was gone. He tested the plane with some gentle maneuvers and concluded that pilot and plane were all right. He landed and was immediately surrounded by his officers. They had witnessed the "impossible" and could attest that their chief had indeed flown on the outside of a giant aerial circle.

The newspapers quickly latched onto the story and, once again, Doolittle found himself the subject of headlines. When he was asked what gave him the idea to try what no other pilot had ever successfully attempted, Doolittle grinned and replied, tongue in cheek, "Don't know why I did it. Just thought of it on the spur of the moment."

It was this sort of quote that gave Doolittle the image of a devil-may-care pilot who would try anything in an airplane at least once. He never gave the impression that he had first put in many hours of careful calculation and practice. He had approached this aeronautical question as a scientist should by taking all the known facts, reasoning what the unknowns were, and theorizing what the outcome should be. There was a certain amount of risk involved, but it was a calculated risk and Doolittle was a master at it. He combined the traits of the daredevil with those of the engineer. However, the newspapers were only interested in playing up the daredevil side of his background. Doolittle had long ago decided that he was not going to try to tell the press what to print. He was interested in extending man's knowledge of flight and he wanted the hard-pressed Air Corps to get proper credit when it was deserved. He would tolerate the front page stories and the exaggerations that over-eager reporters invariably dreamed up. While readers would be amazed, Doolittle would already be planning to conquer something else that was "impossible."

By now the name "Doolittle" was a household name and ranked with a new name, that of Charles A. ("Slim") Lindbergh, who had crossed the Atlantic alone in a single-engine plane a few days before Jimmy had flown the outside loop. Jimmy received hundreds of invitations to fly at air shows, speak at dinners, and appear at social functions. His fame, along with Lindbergh's, spread literally around the globe.

His success on the first South American tour led to an invitation to do it again. So it was that in January 1928 he was granted another leave without pay and climbed aboard a ship in New York, along with Curtiss personnel and two planes—the now-famous P-1 and an O-1, a new observation plane that Curtiss wanted to sell to the Latins.

First stop was Lima, Peru, where Jimmy and William H. McMullen, a Curtiss civilian pilot, put on demonstrations in both planes, first with wheels and then with pontoons. They flew to Bolivia and then Chile and it was here that Jimmy almost met disaster again, although this time it had nothing to do with pisco sours and the officer's club.

There were some British naval officers in Santiago, several of whom were fliers. They had watched the two Americans demonstrate their planes and expressed interest in the pontoon-equipped O-1. "I've flown it before," Commander Bruce Jones, one of the pilots said. "Could I have a go at it again?" he asked.

"Sure," Doolittle said. "You fly it and I'll ride in the rear observer's seat."

Jones started the engine and taxied out into the bay. He had some difficulty taxiing but Doolittle thought it might be because of the choppy water. However, when the British officer gave it full throttle, he knew the man was not as proficient in operating from the water as he should have been. The O-1 swished from side to side as its pilot over-controlled. As speed picked up, the wing tips dipped closer and closer to the wave tops. In the rear seat, without controls, Doolittle was helpless. He knew a crash was coming and he braced himself for the inevitable. The airplane was bouncing through the wave tops and couldn't seem to get airborne. The left wing float caught a wave, the plane swerved, and the left wing sliced into the water. With engine wide open, the O-1 plunged headlong and flipped over onto its back.

The flipping action threw Commander Jones out of his seat and clear of the plane because he had forgotten to fasten his safety belt. Doolittle, strapped in, was upside down in the wreckage. He unbuckled his safety belt and swam clear.

Jones' brother officers on shore had been watching the takeoff and immediately dispatched a motorboat, but Doolittle wasn't sure they would get there in time. Jones had been dazed by the impact and Doolittle saw that he wasn't doing much to save himself. He swam to Jones, held his head out of the water, and reached for the pontoon that had been ripped off and was floating nearby. Between the heavy flying boots and the dead weight of the Englishman, Doolittle wasn't sure he could hold on until the boat got there. To his horror, the pontoon slowly began to sink. Just as it went under, the boat arrived and the two men were fished out. The naval officer was grateful to Doolittle for saving his life; Doolittle was furious at himself for having let the man talk him into flying the plane without any real assurance that he was familiar with its operation on the water.

With only the P-1 left now, Jimmy decided that he would continue the tour by attempting speed records between cities. He flew from Santiago to Buenos Aires in less than six hours, beating his former record by a half hour. From there he flew to Asuncion, Paraguay, setting a record between these two capitals;

then on to Rio de Janeiro across Brazil's great Mato Grosso—the first time such a flight had been attempted. There were no maps available and it was a long and dangerous flight over impenetrable jungle. If he had been forced down, there was little chance that he would ever have been found. Jimmy had extra gas tanks installed and made it in seven hours—another aviation "first."

Each flight and each demonstration made more headlines for "Geemee," and he was acclaimed a hero wherever he went. He was entertained by the presidents and dignitaries of the countries he visited and was made an honorary member of each country's air force. The Bolivians gave him the Order of the Condor, an honor reserved for airmen they admire. The American ambassadors in each country were delighted with the image he portrayed and sent many favorable reports on his tour back to Washington. This one-man goodwill tour had done more to create a favorable impression of the United States in just six months than visits by U.S. Navy fleets and various diplomatic gestures had done for the previous decade. Never again would a single American capture the hearts and the cheers of Latin America with his flying skill.

Jimmy returned to the United States in the summer of 1928 and wondered what the future held for him. Now 31 years old, he was still a first lieutenant. He knew that promotion to a captaincy might still be a long way off, although he now had eleven years' service. Aviation had come a long way in that time, however, and much more could be done. The world had been circled by Air Service pilots in 1924; the Atlantic had been spanned solo in a single-engine plane; mail was being carried along hundreds of miles of air routes; passenger airlines had been started; night flying had become commonplace; speed and altitude records had been steadily upped. What was there left to accomplish that would contribute to air safety and comfort?

In Doolittle's mind, there was much to be done. Flying was still not a reliable means of transportation. Planes couldn't fly in bad weather; pilots who attempted to fly into fog, rain, snow, and ice conditions became tragic statistics in aviation's logbook. Too many pilots had nothing but contempt for weather flying and thought it was a blight on their records if they refused to make an attempt to reach their destination. Too often, pilots would fly into steadily worsening conditions and find themselves in situations where they could not turn back and had only two choices left: bail out or try to luck it through. Those who didn't bail out more often than not ended their careers in a pile of wreckage because their "seat of the pants" instincts were not good enough to overcome the physical fact that they could not possibly tell when they were in straight and level flight when they flew with no outside reference to help them with their balance.

This was the single greatest barrier to safe and efficient flight operations. Some pilots said it would never be solved—that flying would always depend on the man with the greatest skill at flying by instinct. Others said that planes were never meant to fly on schedule and that if people wanted to meet schedules, they should take a train. Anyhow, planes were getting to be so fast that they could almost always overcome the time differential by waiting out the weather and then racing the distance when the weather cleared.

Doolittle's own experience and scientific studies had shown these views to be foolish. He was sure that weather flying could be licked by the design of proper instruments and pilot training in their use. He set this new challenge for himself and embarked on what was to be his greatest contribution to aviation.

He tells about the famous blind flying experiments and provides an interesting insight into this phase of aviation history:

In the early and middle 1920s, the Jones-Barany revolving chair test was given to all military pilots as part of their periodic physical examination for flying. Normally, this test was given with the pilot's eyes open and the flight surgeon looked for variations in times and amount of the rhythmic side-to-side movement of the eyes called *nystagmus*.

In early 1926, Captain (later Colonel) David A. Myers, an outstanding Air Corps flight surgeon, decided to augment the routine test by giving an additional test consisting of several rotations of the chair with the pilot's eyes closed. After the rate of rotation became steady a normal pilot, with eyes closed, could not tell which way he was turning. If the rate of rotation was slowed down and stabilized at a somewhat lower speed, the pilot thought the rotation had been stopped. When the rotation actually was stopped, he thought he was turning in the opposite direction.

The explanation is that man normally maintains his equilibrium by sight, touch, hearing, muscle and vestibular sense. Touch and hearing are not important in flight orientation. By using the three remaining senses he can ascertain and maintain his position, accurately sense the rate and direction of his motion and generally orient himself with relation to the earth.

Sight is by far the most reliable of these three senses and when sight is lost we must get our sense of balance and motion from the muscles and from the fluid movement sensors in the vestibular canals. If an individual is merely displaced, the fluid motions return to zero very rapidly. But if one is rotated, it may take from five to 25 seconds for the fluid motions to stop. During this period an individual can experience the false sense of motion we call *vertigo*. This, of course, explains why early day pilots become completely confused and occasionally spun in and crashed.

Captain (later Colonel) William C. Ocker, an early and extremely competent Air Corps pilot and flight researcher, had long been interested in instrument flying and, in 1918, had tested the then new bank-and-turn indicator. When he took Captain Myers' new "blindfold test" in 1926, his first reaction was that the doctor had played a trick on him or, if not, that his senses had failed him. After further consideration, he decided that here was proof positive that no normal pilot could consistently fly "blind" without reference to instruments.

Ocker, who had considerable experience flying with the bank-and-turn indicator by that time, believed this instrument could correct the pilot's faulty senses. He designed a light-proof "black box" which contained a bank-and-turn indicator and a magnetic compass. This box was mounted on the front of the Jones-Barany chair. The pilot sealed his face against the opening in the box and observed the bank-and-turn indicator and compass. With this piece of equipment he could correctly identify the direction and rate of his rotation. After the rotation stopped and the compass settled down, he could then determine his heading.

Myers and Ocker continued their experiments and the arrangement of the black box and revolving chair were patented and subsequently used in the training of pilots. Later, some pilots were to learn to fly by instruments alone before they learned to fly under normal visual conditions.

In the late '20s and early '30s, Captain Ocker and Lt. (later Colonel) Carl J. Crane collaborated in the study of instrument flying techniques and developed, among other things, a unitary arrangement of instruments which would give the pilot a maximum of useful flight information with a minimum of effort and fatigue. They referred to this as a "flight integrator."

The development of instrument flight owes much to Daniel Guggenheim, one of the great industrialists, philanthropists and citizens of the twentieth century. He was interested in everything that could lead to a fuller life and a better world. One of his great contributions was the Daniel Guggenheim Fund for the Promotion of Aeronautics which was established for the purpose of promoting the advance of the art, science and business of aviation. It proved to be a very effective medium in the accomplishment of that purpose.

The Fund was established in January, 1926, with a grant of $2,500,000. It was to be administered by a Board of Trustees composed of men of "eminence and competence" in cooperation with the Federal Government. Harry Guggenheim, gifted son of Daniel and a World War I naval aviator, was chosen the Fund's president.

From the first, it was understood that flight safety and reliability were important considerations and that one phase of the Fund's work would be to study means of assuring safe and reliable flight despite weather conditions. With this in mind, a special committee of experts was organized to define the problem. A directive was prepared which authorized a study to include the following: dissipation of fog; development of some means whereby flying fields might be located from the air regardless of fog; development of instruments to show accurately the height of airplanes above the ground, to replace barometric instruments which show height above sea level; improvement and perfection of instruments allowing airplanes to fly properly in fog; and the penetration of fog by light rays.

To carry out the program, a Full Flight Laboratory was established at Mitchel Field, Long Island, and furnished with all the necessary facilities and equipment. I was borrowed from the Air

Corps to head the laboratory and was ably assisted by Professor William G. Brown of the Aeronautics Department of MIT.

Our first activity was to study the work previously done on blind landing in fog. We found that tethered balloons had been lined up with the landing field and used with some success in still air and when the fog was not thick. We abandoned this concept immediately because experience had indicated that the fog layer might be very thick and still air could not be depended upon at all times when visibility was restricted as, for example, in a blizzard.

In both England and France, the lead-in cable idea was tried out. In this system, an electrified cable circled the field and led in to a landing. It required very sensitive sensing equipment in the airplane and it was necessary to make a precision turn into the field at low altitude. This turn was extremely difficult to make.

The low frequency radio range had been developed by the Bureau of Standards and the army by that time and was in limited use for aerial navigation. An adaptation of this radio range in the form of a homing beacon seemed to offer the greatest promise for our use. It could also be readily tied in with the radio receiver and other conventional airplane equipment.

Actual blind landings had been attempted with dragging weights and with long tail skids. These either gave an indication upon touching the ground or were rigged to actuate the aircraft control.

The first important expenditures made by the Full Flight Laboratory were for two modern airplanes. One, a Consolidated NY-2 training plane, was to be used in the instrument landing experiments and to test instruments, equipment or devices that might be helpful in overcoming fog flying problems. It had large wings used by the navy for pontoon seaplane training but mounted, in place of the pontoons, a specially reinforced landing gear with long oleo strut action. As a training plane, it had a very high factor of safety, was extremely rugged and was inherently stable about all three axes.

The second plane was a Navy Vought *Corsair* O2U-1. It was to be used for cross-country practice flying and was an excellent airplane for this purpose. It was a fast, good-flying airplane, but not as rugged as the NY-2.

Lieutenant (later Brigadier General) Ben S. Kelsey was made available by the Air Corps as flight assistant and safety pilot. When flights under the hood were made, it was necessary in the interest of safety to have another pilot in the airplane to look out for other planes and also to make sure that the pilot under the hood did not get into trouble due to instrument or equipment failure.

As the preliminary practice flights progressed, it soon became apparent that even with the very stable and sturdy NY-2, the available instruments were not adequate. For determining heading when maneuvering and when landing, the compass, due to the northerly turning error, was entirely unsatisfactory and the bank-and-turn indicator, though excellent for its purpose, was more a qualitative than a quantitative measuring instrument. Also, at the moment of touchdown in a blind landing, it was imperative that the wings be level with the ground. This was not easy to assure, particularly when the wind was gusty. What was needed was an accurate, reliable and easy-to-read instrument showing exact direction of heading and precise attitude of the aircraft, particularly for the initial and final stages of blind landings.

Two German artificial horizon instruments—the Anschutz and the Gyrorector—were studied but were not deemed entirely satisfactory. I sketched a rough picture of the dial for an instrument which I thought would do the job and showed it to Elmer Sperry, Sr., a great engineer and inventor who headed the Sperry Gyroscope Co. It was, in substance, the face of a directional gyro superimposed on an artificial horizon.

Mr. Sperry advised that a single gyroscopic instrument could be built but recommended, for simplicity of construction, two separate instruments. I agreed, so Mr. Sperry assigned his son, Elmer, Jr., to work with us and be responsible for their design and fabrication. Out of this work came the Sperry artificial horizon and the directional gyroscope which still, with their improved descendants, are on the instrument panel of every airliner and military plane today.

As time progressed, literally hundreds of blind and simulated blind landings were made. To make a landing, the plane was put into a glide at 60 mph, with some power on, and flown directly into the ground. Although this was about 15 mph above stalling speed, the landing gear absorbed the shock of landing and if the angle of glide was just right, the airplane didn't even bounce. Actually, after a while, it was possible to make consistently perfect landings by this method. To assure just the right amount of power in the glide, a mark was placed at the proper place on the throttle quadrant.

Excellent cooperation was obtained from the companies and individuals we worked with during this period. Among them were the

Pioneer Instrument Co., the Taylor Instrument Co., the Radio Corporation of America and the Bell Telephone Laboratories, who installed the modern radio transmitter and provided miniature earphones with molded plugs. Very valuable help was also received from the Bureau of Standards who designed and installed most of the ground and airborne radio navigation equipment.

It was during the radio phase of our tests that we concluded that while aural signals were satisfactory for rough aerial navigation, it would be much better if we had a visual indicator in the cockpit for the precise directional control needed during the final phase of blind landings. The Bureau of Standards, working with the Airways and Radio Division of the Department of Commerce, designed a semi-portable two-leg range, which was used as a homing beacon and a fan-type marker beacon. The homing range was installed on the west side of Mitchel Field. The marker beacon sat along the leg of the homing range and was located on the east side of the field.

In the plane cockpit was an indicator connected to the radio set consisting of a pair of vibrating reeds. If the pilot was to the right of the radio beam, the left reed vibrated more vigorously. If on course, both reeds vibrated through the same arc. As the plane approached the radio station, the amplitude of vibration increased. A single reed started to vibrate as the fan type marker beacon was approached. It reached maximum amplitude then quickly dropped to zero when the plane was directly overhead, rapidly built up to maximum again, and then tapered down as the plane pulled away. The homing range indicator also had a distinct null (period of silence) in the headset when the airplane was directly over the range station.

As the tests progressed, the instrumentation and equipment was continually improved until toward the end of 1929, during the final stages of the flight tests, there were a total of 11 instruments, besides the normal engine instruments, being used.

Considerable thought was given to the location or arrangement of each instrument in order to facilitate reading and reduce pilot fatigue. Fatigue led to errors and piloting errors could not be tolerated in instrument landings.

During this period, while flying the O2U-1, I experienced an extreme example of a cross-country bad weather flight. I took off from Buffalo, New York and headed for Mitchel Field. It was night and the weather was fair and improving at Buffalo but marginal to the south and east. This was to be a difficult flight but possible—just the sort of thing required to establish flight "limitations." In a pinch, I could return to Buffalo any time up to the point where nearly half of the gas supply was used up.

I well realized by then that the pilot who flew within his limitations would probably live to a ripe old age, whereas the pilot who flew beyond them would not. I also knew that different pilots had different limitations.

This was pointed up in my beginning days as a test pilot at McCook Field. At that time there were few facilities and little ground equipment to do environmental testing on new airborne devices. Consequently, we had to test them in flight and spent many hours flying around the Dayton area to see how a new device held up under the accelerations, vibrations and changes in temperature and pressure experienced while flying.

One of our pilots, Lt. Alex Pearson, always spent these hours practicing precision flying—holding constant speed and altitude. As a result, he became extremely proficient and could fly a better speed course or do a smoother sawtooth climb than any of the rest of us.

I spent the hours flying low in the vicinity of McCook Field and on the main air routes in and out memorizing the terrain. I knew every high building, tree, silo, windmill, radio tower and high tension line in the area. I could, therefore, fly in or under adverse weather safely when other equally experienced pilots didn't fly. This was not because I was a better or more daring pilot than my colleagues. Constant practice had just extended my limitations. The trick was to learn your personal limitations, then gradually expand them but never go beyond them.

I thought I was being pretty sharp but the Commanding Officer, learning that I frequently flew in the area when other pilots did not, thought differently. Unaware of my training plan, he removed me from the job of chief pilot in the flying section—advised me that I didn't have judgment enough to be a pilot—and assigned me to the airplane section as an aeronautical engineer.

All of these things went through my mind as the weather deteriorated on the flight from Buffalo. I planned to fly "contact" all the way and avoid any weather, so in order to avoid the mountains, I took route from Buffalo by way of Rochester, Syracuse, Albany and then down the Hudson River. There was no problem getting to Albany but from there on the ceiling and visibility became marginal.

I soon passed "the point of no return" and no longer had gas enough to make it back to Buffalo.

At one point as I flew lower and lower, I found it expedient to slow down and hover with the left wing of the plane over a brightly-lit, southbound passenger train traveling along the east side of the Hudson. Presently it went through a cut and wiped me off. This was too hazardous, so I left the train behind and followed the river bank. I thought about landing on the parade ground at West Point but abandoned this idea since the weather remained flyable—barely. Upon reaching the lights of New York City, the ceiling and visibility improved slightly. I flew south to the Battery hoping to reach Mitchel Field from there, but the East River and the area to the south was socked in so I could not go on. I tried to get to Governors Island and land on the drill field but there it was also completely covered by fog.

I then turned back up the Hudson intending to land on the Yonkers Golf Course which I knew well, but the fog was below the river bank. Turning back, I then thought of crash landing in Battery Park. Just as I was about to set the plane down, a chap ran out into the middle of the park and waved me off. He apparently thought I mistook it for a flying field.

It is interesting to note that the George Washington Bridge across the Hudson was under construction at that time. There were as yet no suspension cables or other horizontal structures. Only the great vertical piers on each side of the river had been completed. I had passed the east pier three times without seeing it.

About this time it appeared that a crash landing in the river might be necessary so I removed my parachute in order to be able to swim ashore.

The water, on closer inspection, looked uninviting so I decided on a final try—this time for Newark Airport—and headed across the Hudson. As soon as I crossed and the lights south of Jersey City appeared, I knew this last chance wasn't practical.

I pulled up into the fog and climbed through it. It was only about a thousand feet thick and crystal clear above. My new plan was to fly west until past the populated part of the metropolitan area and then jump. I didn't know how much time was left but the gas gauge had been fluttering around zero for some time. I noted about this time that my parachute harness was off and [I] promptly put it on.

Somewhere near Kenilworth, New Jersey, I saw a revolving bea-

con through a hole in the fog and a flat-looking area adjacent to it
with no lights. Hoping that it might be an emergency field or at least
an open area, although realizing that it might be a woods or a lake,
I turned the landing lights on and dove through the hole to scout the
area. The bottom of the fog was still very low and I tore the left
lower wing badly on a tree top. The airplane still flew, although almost completely out of gasoline, so I returned to the most likely
spot and crash landed.

I took the impact by wrapping the left wing around a tree trunk
near the ground. The O2U-1 was completely washed out but I was
not even scratched or bruised.

The moral of the story is that had I been flying the NY-2 with its
blind flying equipment and the Laboratory radio station had been
alerted at Mitchel, it would have been a routine cross-country flight
with "no sweat."

The flight pointed up to me the importance of constant radio
communications between an aircraft and the ground and the need
for frequent and accurate weather reports by radio during flight. It
also showed the desirability to mark emergency fields for night landings. Later, green lights were used on the opposite side of the flash-
ing beacons to indicate a landing field.

This flight also brought home the fact that weather flying was a
function of airplane characteristics, ground facilities, airborne equipment and instruments, procedures, pilot skill and his specialized
knowledge of the local aids to air navigation, the terrain and the
weather conditions to be expected in a landing area.

At this stage, it was important that a better altimeter be developed so a pilot would have a precise measure of altitude when
approaching for a landing. The conventional barometric altimeters
of the day measured, at best, to the nearest fifty or one hundred feet.
It would be handy if an altimeter were available that, near the
ground, would measure to ten or even five feet.

The Kollsman Instrument Co. developed such an instrument and
I was very pleased, on August 30, 1929, to take Mr. Paul Kollsman
and his new instrument up on its first test flight in the second O2U
which was purchased after the crash of the first. Mr. Kollsman held
the sensitive altimeter in his lap during the flight and it performed
perfectly. We promptly installed it in the NY-2.

What made this instrument so valuable then was that it had two
hands and a multiplication factor of twenty between them. The

One of Doolittle's most significant contributions to aeronautics was his blind flying "first." Flying a Consolidated NY-2 (above) with a hood over the cockpit, he was the first man in history to take off, fly a course, and land without ever seeing outside the cockpit. (*Photo courtesy of the National Air and Space Museum*)

The cockpit of the Consolidated NY-2 trainer with several of the different types of instruments Doolittle used in blind flight experiments. Although crude by today's standards, these instruments marked the beginning of the end of "seat-of-the-pants" flying.

fast-moving hand made one complete revolution for each 1,000 feet change in altitude which meant a movement of about 5/32 inch for 20 feet altitude. This was an order of magnitude more accurate than earlier altimeters.

We experimented with sonic and radio altimeters, fog penetration lights and fog dispersal methods. None of these experiments were really successful at the time. One fog dispersal experiment using a giant blow torch seemed like it had possibilities, however, and we encouraged its inventor to install his equipment at Mitchel to wait for a foggy day. The morning of September 24, 1929 was perfect for such a trial and Mr. Guggenheim and all our associates were hurriedly called to witness the demonstration. The equipment was fired up even though some of those we wanted to see it, including Mr. Guggenheim, couldn't get there quickly. We were afraid the fog would burn off so we fired up the equipment, but the fog did not disperse.

Though we were all disappointed, we were there and the fog was there, so I decided to make a real fog flight. The NY-2 was pushed out of the hangar and warmed up. The ground radios were manned and the radio beacons turned on. I taxied out and took off. Came through the fog at about 500 feet and made a wide swing coming around into landing position. By the time I landed ten minutes after take-off the fog had just started to lift.

About this time, Mr. Guggenheim, along wih several other people, arrived so we decided to do an "official" under-the-hood flight. I'd just made a real flight in the fog so [I] wanted to go alone but Mr. Guggenheim insisted that Ben Kelsey be taken along as safety pilot. The fog had lifted considerably by this time and he was afraid there might be other aircraft in the vicinity.

We both got into the plane and the hood over my cockpit was tightly closed. I taxied out and took off toward the west in a gradual climb. At about 1,000 feet, I leveled off and made a 180-degree turn to the left, flew several miles, then made another left turn. The airplane was now properly lined up on the west leg of the Mitchel range so I started a gradual descent. I leveled off at 200 feet and flew level until I passed the fan marker on the east side of the field. From this point, I flew the plane down to the ground using the instrument landing procedure we had developed. However, despite all my previous practice, the approach and landing were sloppy.

The whole flight lasted only 15 minutes. So far as I know, this was the first time an airplane had been taken off, flown over a set course and landed by instruments alone. This was just ten months and three weeks from the first test flight of the NY-2.

At the end of 1929 the Fund trustees, feeling that we had made the necessary initial contribution, and believing that further development could better be carried out by other organizations, disbanded the organization. The Full Flight Laboratory went out of existence with the Fund and the NY-2 was moved to Wright Field for further use in instrument landing experimentation.

The fifteen-minute flight of Jimmy Doolittle that early September morning marked the end of the "seat of the pants" era of aviation. And while it did not represent the final solution to the problem of flying solely by the use of instruments, it did lay the essential groundwork for the sophisticated blind flying techniques used today. It was Jimmy Doolittle who had pushed back the frontier of flying another notch. Characteristically, he began to look for another challenge as the third decade of flight was nearing its end.

9. Twice a Caterpillar

Dᴜʀɪɴɢ ᴛʜᴇ Pʀᴇʟɪᴍɪɴᴀʀʏ Pᴇʀɪᴏᴅ before the actual blind flight experiments in the fall of 1929, an incident occurred that nearly spelled the end for Doolittle. The National Air Races were scheduled to be held in Cleveland that year and Jimmy couldn't resist the opportunity to put on an acrobatic show in the Curtiss P-1 *Hawk* as part of the festivities. He had been busy with the fog-flying tests and had not had sufficient time to practice. However, he was not about to take up a fast fighter plane through his routine after several months of flying a slow trainer without practicing first. Since he arrived late on the day before he was scheduled to perform, he arose early the next morning, strapped himself in his plane, and took off.

Climbing to altitude, he went through his usual set of maneuvers until he felt that he had recovered his touch on the sensitive *Hawk* controls. Last on his practice program was a power dive, which he began by making a half roll and then pulling through.

The plane responded magnificently, but as Doolittle leveled off one wing sheared and made a terrifying noise as it ripped off. The plane cartwheeled through space and then started to spin wildly out of control. With great difficulty, Jimmy fought off the weight of centrifugal force and jumped out. He pulled the rip-cord of his parachute and floated serenely to earth while the plane smashed itself to bits in the Ohio countryside.

An army press release put out a few days later tells of the incident:

Lieutenant James H. Doolittle, the well-known Army flier, is evidently a firm believer of the adage that "Brevity is the soul of wit." There is such a thing, however, as being too brief. Lieutenant Doolittle, who joined the Caterpillar Club September 1 by reason of the fact that he was forced to make a parachute jump when his plane disintegrated in the air while practicing acrobatics for an exhibition before a crowd of 150,000 people at the National Air Races at Cleveland, is the 150th airman in this country to join this mythical organization. The official report of his experience, which every member of the Army Air Corps is required to make after an emergency parachute jump, was received today by the Chief of the Air Corps. It indicates far better than words can describe his character as an aviator and a reason why he is one of the most proficient experimental and test pilots in the Army Air Corps.

Army officials at the Air Races had been anxiously waiting his return in order to service his plane for the exhibition flight when he walked into Army headquarters with his parachute under his arm and said: "Gentlemen, I guess I'll have to borrow another plane." This was the first intimation received of his jump.

Within the prescribed thirty minutes Lieutenant Doolittle taxied his borrowed plane to the starting line, took off at the wave of the flag, and staged as beautiful a demonstration of acrobatic flying as had ever been witnessed. The official report of his emergency jump indicates that to him such an incident is just a part of the day's work and nothing to get excited about. In submitting an official report on an emergency jump, the person making the jump is required to answer in detail eleven questions, covering place, date, and time of the jump; the type of aircraft used; whether the plane was under control; description of method of leaving the aircraft; complete and accurate account of the feelings and reactions of the jump during and immediately after the jump; weather conditions at the time; and what ill effects or injury was sustained.

Lieutenant Doolittle used just thirty-eight words in his report.

Under the question, "Cause for the emergency jump" he states: "Wings Broke." No answer was given under the question, "Feeling and reaction of the jump." Describing his method of leaving the aircraft, he just states: "Thrown out."

A newspaperman who happened to witness Lieutenant Doolittle's jump and drove over to help him to his feet when he had landed on the ground, asked the popular Air Corps officer what his reactions were. Lieutenant Doolittle replied: "I am glad it happened. I have always wanted to be forced to jump. I have almost had to go over the side several times, but this time there wasn't any other choice. I had to!"

This latest event in the busy life of Jimmy Doolittle earned him an award that no man seeks deliberately. He was made a member of the Caterpillar Club, an organization made up of persons who have leaped out of planes to save their lives. It derives its name from the caterpillar that spins the silk from which parachutes are made. Those who qualify are presented a small jewelled pin by the Irvin Parachute Company. For Doolittle, it was only the first time he would earn it.

The end of the blind flying experiments in 1929 marked a crossroads in the crowded life of Jimmy Doolittle. In spite of his accomplishments, he was still a first lieutenant and had been one since July 1, 1920. Promotions were so slow in the peacetime Air Corps that he had no idea when or if he would ever be promoted to captain. Some of the men commissioned prior to World War I had been in grade as long as seventeen years before being promoted to the next higher rank.

The fame that had come to Doolittle had also brought job offers in private industry. With a wife and two sons to care for, a first lieutenant's pay of about $200 per month did not match the standard of living that the now-famous flier wanted for his family. They had been able to accumulate a small savings, a few household items, and nothing else. The only homes they had known were those the army had provided. However, Jimmy loved the army and was grateful for the opportunities that had come his way. He had made the most of them. He felt he had more to offer the science of aviation and began to see that private industry would give him new opportunities that were not possible in the Air Corps—especially with a national economic depression imminent.

Jimmy made his decision in December 1929. He had received an offer from the Shell Oil Company to join its staff in St. Louis and lend his name and background to their aviation division. He resigned his regular commission on February 15, 1930, but asked to be commissioned in the Air Corps Reserve. His request was granted, and to his surprise he was commissioned a major, skipping the rank of captain.

The day before Jimmy was to return to civilian life, he was given a party in New York City by the many friends in the business and military worlds his life had touched. Many newspaper writers were there, too, for they had come to like this man whose name certainly did not fit his many accomplishments.

Jimmy was overwhelmed by the fact that so many people would turn out to wish him well in a new career. He didn't say much that night except that he had bought a plane to do some flying for Shell and that his contract would allow him to engage in other aviation activities. He had retired from the Air Corps, he said, because of "advanced age," but no one who heard him that night really expected him to quit racing and acrobatic flying.

Part of the deal with Shell included the purchase of a Lockheed *Vega*, a fast, barrel-shaped monoplane that would hold four people comfortably and flash along at better than two hundred mph. Jimmy flew it from the Lockheed factory in California to Long Island and intended to fly Jo and the two boys in it from New York to St. Louis when he was officially released from the army. The night of February 16 was cold and snow began to blow across the runway at Mitchel Field. But Doolittle had promised to be at work in St. Louis next day and was determined to keep that promise.

Bundling Jo and the boys into the trim white *Vega*, he warmed up the engine and taxied out through the blowing snow to takeoff position. The *Vega*, heavily-loaded with the Doolittle family belongings, seemed ready so Jimmy gave it the throttle and started down the runway. But the 425-horsepower engine couldn't seem to develop the power to get the load airborne. The snowdrifts held the wheels back while the engine strained at full power.

Suddenly, the left wheel caught a snowdrift and jerked the plane sideways. There was a wrenching sound and the landing gear buckled. The *Vega* lay in a snowdrift beside the runway like a crippled bird. Fortunately, no one was hurt but the door was jammed and the four Doolittles were imprisoned inside until a crash crew extricated them.

While Jo and the boys were driven back to base operations, Doolittle surveyed the damage to the new plane and was heartbroken. Besides the landing gear, the left wing was smashed and the gas tank was punctured. He was disgusted with himself and felt it was a very poor way to begin a new life as a civilian flier.

The Shell people did not feel as bad as Doolittle and quickly had the plane repaired. However, Jimmy reported to the St. Louis headquarters by train—the worst fate he could imagine.

Shortly after getting on the Shell payroll, Curtiss-Wright officials asked Shell if they could borrow his services for a tour of Europe to demonstrate four different types of their planes— pursuit, training, reconnaissance, and observation. Twenty-one countries were on the itinerary, beginning in Greece and ending in Switzerland. In April, accompanied by three Army fliers on loan, Jimmy sailed for Athens along with the planes and mechanics.

As could be expected, Jimmy's job was to put on an air show the Europeans would not soon forget. He did. He would take off and put any one of the four types of planes through a dizzying series of loops, rolls, dives, and acrobatics that amazed the crowds wherever the group went.

For Doolittle the experience included more than flying. In the 8,000-mile tour, he met many military airmen and was shown the latest in aviation developments in the countries he visited. He was particularly concerned about Germany, which was putting unusual emphasis on increasing the speed of its planes—a sure preliminary to making better military aircraft, which they were forbidden to do according to their treaty with the winning Allies after World War I. From the new aircraft designs he saw, Jimmy felt an urge to hurry back to the United States and encourage more racing by Americans. He knew that racing planes, just as racing automobiles, leads to continual improvements in engines, fuels, lubricants, and design of the machines themselves. In addition, racing invariably leads to safety improvements.

Because of what he saw, Jimmy decided to devote the next three years to racing while working for Shell. Although he knew his job was to sell gasoline for his company, he convinced his superiors that they should authorize the purchase of some of the fastest planes available for racing and testing. Naturally, he would do most of the flying in them.

But Doolittle didn't want the company to take an unreasonable financial risk. With the family savings, he bought a wrecked Beech *Travelair* monoplane (which the press had dubbed the "Mystery Ship") for his own experimentation. As it was put back into flying shape, Doolittle ordered modifications in the fuselage, which he hoped would make it the world's fastest plane.

Doolittle and an associate checked the plane carefully and deemed it ready for a real workout—Doolittle style. Proud of the trim, sleek racing version, he invited some friends to see it perform, including his son, Jimmy, Jr. Takeoff was smooth and the plane climbed like a rocket. After testing the plane in routine maneuvers at altitude, Doolittle made a speed run across the field. The air speed indicator needle crept up, up, up and steadied at nearly three hundred miles per hour. Doolittle was pleased, but as he leveled out an ominous metal-wrenching sound rose above the engine noise. The plane began to vibrate badly and its pilot knew that his prized possession was beginning to break apart. He nosed up and pulled back on the throttle, but it was too late. The aileron control that he had personally redesigned wouldn't stand the strain and the wings began to disintegrate.

There was only one thing to do and Doolittle did it. He unfastened his safety belt and pushed himself out of the seat. Just as he did, the wing ripped off and the plane careened wildly out of control. With a sudden burst of strength, he pulled himself over the side of the cockpit and grabbed the ripcord of his parachute. His split-second reaction and the slipstream of the faltering plane enabled the parachute to snap open quickly in spite of the fact that he was only about five hundred feet above the ground. The 'chute popped open and his feet hit the ground in a one-two count. He had survived one of the lowest jumps ever made. His success earned him membership in the famed Caterpillar Club for the second time.

Although this experience had almost cost him his life, what bothered Doolittle most was what had caused the mishap. His best drawing board calculations had not been good enough. An airplane still had to be flown to see if it could withstand the stresses that were intended. Would it always be so? Doolittle hoped not.

Undaunted by the near-miss with death, Doolittle worked with E. M. ("Matty") Laird, a manufacturer of racing planes, and produced a plane called the Laird *Super Solution*. A biplane, it was powered by a 510-hp Wright *Wasp* engine and had an enclosed undercarriage which gave it a clean, sleek appearance when it was airborne. It was Doolittle's intention to enter it in the Bendix Race—an annual free-for-all transcontinental dash from Burbank, California, to Cleveland, Ohio, the site of the 1931 · National Air Races.

Just after midnight on September 4, 1931, eight pilots chafed on the ground at Burbank waiting for the weatherman to give them the green light. All but two were flying Lockheed planes. Besides Doolittle's Laird the other non-Lockheed was a *Travelair R*. At 2:30 A.M., the signal was given and the pilots took off at timed intervals to prevent collisions.

From the start, it didn't appear that there was any race. The *Super Solution* leaped out in front and streaked eastward. After stops at Albuquerque and Kansas City, Doolittle landed at Cleveland in a light, drizzling rain. Time: 9 hours, 10 minutes— better by four minutes than the next pilot, who was flying a Lockheed *Orion*.

Jimmy won the $15,000 Bendix Trophy Race at Cleveland in 1931. Not content with this victory, he refueled quickly and took off for New York to break the transcontinental record set the year before by Capt. Frank Hawkes. He is shown above departing Cleveland for the final leg. The plane is a Laird *Super Solution*, powered by a Pratt & Whitney *Wasp Junior*, which developed about 510 horsepower. (*Photos courtesy of the U.S. Air Force*)

But, to the amazement of the Cleveland crowd, Doolittle was not satisfied with stopping at Cleveland. He had an idea that he could set a new coast-to-coast record and beat the then-current mark of 12 hours, 25 minutes set by Frank Hawks the year before. If he could, he would get an extra $2,500 which the Bendix Trophy people said they would add to the prize of $7,500 for winning the race.

Helping the ground crew gas his plane and refusing the sandwich Jo Doolittle handed up to him, Jimmy was eager to go on. He jumped into the cockpit, fired up the *Wasp* engine, and headed the Laird toward Newark, New Jersey. The flight path was directly into a line of thunderstorms.

Fighting fatigue and the weather, the determined Doolittle bored on through and touched down at Newark just 11 hours and 16 minutes after leaving Burbank. It was another victory but the incredible Doolittle was not yet through flying. Gassing up again, he posed briefly for newspaper photographers and was back in the air within an hour bound for Cleveland. Later that afternoon, he flew on to St. Louis to attend a party given by his Shell colleagues to celebrate his Bendix win. In that one-day period, he had flown over 3,500 miles, set a national coast-to-coast speed record, and won a prized speed trophy. In addition, he had scored another aviation "first"—he had been the first to span the continent in less than twelve hours, just as, exactly nine years before, to the day, he had been first to do it under twenty-four hours. September 4, 1931, had been a great day in the life of Jimmy Doolittle and a great day for Aviation.

Shell Oil Company's decision to hire Jimmy Doolittle to sell aviation products was a good one. He was front-page news wherever he went now and invariably the news accounts would refer to him as "Jimmy Doolittle of the Shell Oil Co." After winning the Bendix Trophy, his exploits were always thereafter connected with Shell gasoline and lubricants. He was the best advertisement the company ever had.

To keep his name and the name of Shell before the public, it was decided that Jimmy should be allowed to make an entire

Doolittle poses for photographers at St. Louis, Missouri, after setting the
Mexico City-to-New York City record of 6 hours, 33 minutes on October
26, 1931. (*Photo courtesy of the National Archives*)

series of record-setting flights between cities in North America. Beginning shortly after the Bendix Race in September, 1931, he established records between St. Louis and Indianapolis and St. Louis and Chicago. He reenacted the first airmail flight out of St. Louis, carrying a pouch of five thousand airmail letters and cutting the old time in half to dramatize how much flying speeds had increased.

In mid-October, Jimmy flew to Ottawa, Canada. He announced that he was going to fly to Mexico City via Washington, D.C., because no record had ever been set between the three capitals. With only a small group of mechanics and Canadian officials present, Doolittle fired up a new model of the Laird *Super Solution* and took off. In 2 hours and 20 minutes he landed at Washington, gassed up, and was away thirty minutes later. Dropping in at Birmingham, Alabama, in less than two hours, he was off again after only a seven-minute gas stop. Landing in Corpus Christi, Texas, for a sixteen-minute gas stop, he was up, up and away for the Mexican capital and landed at the national airport there in 11 hours and 45 minutes elapsed flying time after takeoff from Ottawa.

The Mexicans gave Jimmy a warm hero's welcome in true Latin style. He was wined and dined for a full week, but this did not deter him from thinking up new records to set. He told the Mexican press that he planned to establish a record from Mexico City to St. Louis and he did. With landings at Brownsville, Texas, and Shreveport, Louisiana, he touched down at the St. Louis airport only 6 hours and 35 minutes after taking off from the high-altitude (7,500 feet) Mexican capital.

The American public followed fast-moving Doolittle's every flight with great interest. His flying achievements were covered in practically every American newspaper at some time or another and his grinning face was seen more times than any other American. Writers began to speculate on what records he would attempt next. One wrote that he suspected Doolittle merely looked at the official record statistics of the National Aeronautic Association and was determined to go after them all, one by one.

When the new year—1932—began, Jimmy decided on a new type of flight. He took off from St. Louis for Cuba with Jo Doolittle and two other passengers. They landed at Jacksonville, Florida, for breakfast, had lunch in Havana, and flew to Miami for supper after Jimmy had put on a demonstration of his plane for Cuban officials. This flight made news, not because of the speed he attained between each city, but because of its casualness. Four people decided to have a relaxed few hours of flight and go to Cuba. They did. No problems. No emergencies. No complicated arrangements. The point Doolittle made was a simple one: flying was now becoming safe—so safe that flights like this one were no longer a dream but a fact. They could be made in effortless comfort. Writers predicted that businessmen would soon be able to save valuable time with company-owned planes. The whole world would soon be airborne.

Doolittle merely smiled at these perceptions. This was what he had wanted to prove and he had done it without actually saying so. His flights focused attention on aviation where public support was badly needed because, in those days, too many people regarded flying as only for the foolhardy. "If Man was meant to fly," some people said, "he would have been provided with wings." Doolittle's flights showed that Man's ingenuity had indeed provided those wings and that he was meant to fly after all.

Although it did seem that Doolittle was about to run out of new ways to capture public attention for Shell, someone came up with a new slant. Why not fly over all the routes covered by George Washington in his lifetime in a single day?

Doolittle looked over the itinerary and decided that it was possible. It would cover fourteen states—from Maine to North Carolina and west to Ohio. Commemorative mail would be carried and dropped along the 2,600-mile route. Miss Anne Madison Washington, an attractive, middle-aged descendant of the first President, would go along, plus an official of the Aeronautical Chamber of Commerce. It was to be billed as the George Washington Bicentennial Airplane Flight and would commemorate the 157th anniversary of the founding of the U.S. Postal Service.

As the date neared, press interest picked up, especially when Doolittle was nearly killed only a week before at Evansville, Indiana, in a crash landing. Fortunately, he was unhurt and had no intention of disappointing those who had planned the flight.

On a warm July morning, Jimmy warmed up his Lockheed *Orion* monoplane, loaded the mail and Miss Washington aboard, and took off from Washington, D.C., for New York. It was Miss Washington's first flight but she wasn't nervous when it was explained to her just who the pilot was. The two, now joined by Mr. A. F. Maple, left New York for Boston, then to Kittery, Maine, the official starting point for the flight.

The yellow monoplane winged low over the village of Kittery just as dawn was breaking. Doolittle circled once, dropped down, and threw a mail pouch out the door. He swung south and repeated the mailbag throwing at Portsmouth, New Hampshire, Providence, Rhode Island, New Haven, Connecticut, and Morristown, New Jersey. Climbing above the smoky haze covering the metropolitan areas, Doolittle circled over Trenton and Camden, New Jersey, and then Valley Forge—three places with special significance in Washington's life.

At 9 A.M., the Lockheed landed at Washington, D.C., for gas. Fifteen minutes later, it was headed for Mount Vernon, Fredericksburg, Wakefield, and Yorktown, more names with special meaning. The next mail was dropped at Sunbury, North Carolina. Turning north again, Doolittle flew over Christiansburg and Winchester, Virginia, then northwest to Fort Necessity and Pittsburgh, Pennsylvania, where another gas stop was made.

Leaving Pittsburgh, the *Orion* flew to Point Pleasant and Pomeroy, Ohio, the point farthest west that Washington ever traveled. Heading northeast now, Doolittle flew to Fort Le Boeuf, near Waterford, Pennsylvania, then to Rome, New York, for a dusk mail drop. From there, it was on to Crown Point, Ticonderoga, Albany, and a final mail drop at West Point, home of the U.S. Military Academy. At 10:15 P.M., the trio of tired travelers stepped out of the plane at Newark. The flight had covered 2,610 miles and had taken 15 hours and 40 minutes—the precise time that Doolittle had figured when he planned it.

While the flight may have seemed like a publicity stunt to most people, it proved another point for the future for airmail and passenger-carrying airlines. It *was* possible for a pilot to navigate to a number of scattered towns, drop mail at any of them, and do it on a reliable schedule. And it could be done with passengers aboard.

The implications were clear. Flying had truly reached that point in time when mail and people could go by air—safely and reliably.

10. Never Another Pylon

JUST AS THE MONTH of May means auto races at Indianapolis, in the 1930s September meant the National Air Races at Cleveland. In 1932 there was great excitement about the annual events there because of Doolittle's exploits and the mounting desire by pilots all over the world to compete for the fame and fortune that went with winning the various events.

In the summer of 1932 Jimmy announced his intention to enter the Burbank-to-Cleveland Bendix Race again and hoped to lower the record he had set the year before. The Laird *Super Solution* was rebuilt to hold a larger, more powerful engine and some modifications were made on the fuselage. Most notable of the changes was the retractable landing gear which would fold up inside the belly of the fast racer. The new combination, he thought, would give him fifty to sixty more miles per hour.

But fate was not to allow him to find out what the new version would really do. On August 23, 1932, while flying it for the first time at Wichita, he found that he could not wind down the gear. He wrote a note about the difficulty and dropped it to the ground crew: SOMETHING WRONG LANDING GEAR. I CAN GET THREE AND ONE-HALF TURNS BOTH WAYS.

IF YOU HAVE SUGGESTIONS, WRITE THEM ON SIDE OF PLANE AND COME UP. OTHERWISE, WILL USE UP GAS AND BELLY IN.

After a hurried consultation among the mechanics, one of them wrote on the side of a plane: ZOOM RIGHT. ZOOM LEFT. POWER DIVE. A pilot flew alongside Doolittle, who acknowledged with a wave and began a series of dives and pullouts to the right, left, and straight ahead to try to dislodge the gear. He tried for two hours, but nothing worked. When his gas was nearly gone, he entered the landing pattern and made a wheels up landing. The grinding of belly and propeller against the runway made Doolittle sick inside. He was unhurt but a gear-up landing meant the end of his plans to attempt a second win of the Bendix Trophy—or so he thought.

Just as his exploits had made headlines, so did his misfortunes. The wire services carried the story about his bad luck with the premature announcement that Doolittle would be unable to compete. But the press was wrong. Offers began to be phoned and telegraphed to Jimmy in Wichita from owners and manufacturers all over the country who wanted to loan him their racing planes.

One of the offers was from Russell Boardman, who offered Doolittle a *Gee Bee* R-1 racing plane, considered by many pilots to be the most dangerous airplane ever built. Boardman had been hospitalized after a crash in it but the plane was ready to fly again before Boardman was. Jimmy flew to Springfield, Massachusetts, to see about it.

As he walked around the rebuilt *Gee Bee*, he was amazed that such an airplane could fly. It looked like a barrel. Short, stubby wings seemed to be attached as an afterthought. There wasn't much of a vertical fin and there was just barely enough cockpit space for a small boy, and it was located just in front of the vertical stabilizer. Doolittle thought, no wonder it had the reputation of being an unstable beast in flight. It would be fast, no doubt about that, but it would be tough to handle in turns. Stability had been sacrificed in order to get maximum speed.

Because of its small fuel supply, Doolittle knew he couldn't

enter the Bendix cross-country race, but the *Gee Bee* wasn't designed for long-distance flying anyway. He announced that he
would fly it in the Thompson Trophy Race instead.

To qualify for the Thompson event, each pilot had to fly over
the course at an average speed of two hundred miles per hour. It
would be no problem for Doolittle but, as always, he wanted to
know his airplane thoroughly before he flew it at its maximum
potential. He recalls:

> I flew the *Gee Bee* from Springfield to Cleveland. It was the
> "touchiest" plane I had ever been in. At Cleveland, I took it up
> to practice pylon turns but climbed up to 5,000 feet. It's a good
> thing I did. That airplane did two snap rolls before I could get it
> under control. Had I practiced that near the ground instead of at
> 5,000 feet, I would have been dead.

When it came time for the qualifying run, Jimmy zoomed over
the course four times and felt sure that he had flown faster than
he ever had before in his life. He had. His average speed was
293.93 miles per hour—a new world landplane record. Unfortunately, the record could not be counted. According to the rules
of the National Aeronautic Association, any record attempt had
to be "sanctioned"—that is, approved in advance so that NAA
officials could install barographs to verify that a pilot did not get
above 1300 feet while making his runs. Jimmy was disappointed
when he found that he could not claim a record. When ques-
tioned about it, he told the press that he thought such details
would be handled by the race officials. "I'm the pilot," he told
the press. "I thought the officials running the race would have
things set up properly in case someone did set a record. It's their
business, not mine. A pilot has all he can do to fly his ship."

Thinking about it overnight, Jimmy asked that the proper arrangements be made and a barograph installed so that he could
try again. He didn't equal his old record this time, but did beat
the previous record set eight years earlier by a French pilot by
four miles per hour. However, another rule prevented this claim
from being called "official." A record-setting flight had to better
an old record by *five* miles an hour!

The *Gee Bee* was probably one of the most dangerous aircraft ever used for racing. With practically no vertical fin, it was extremely unstable. Note the pilot's cockpit just forward of the vertical fin. Powered by a Pratt & Whitney *Wasp* engine developing about 800 horsepower, the top speed flown by any pilot was about 275 mph. (*Photo courtesy of the U.S. Air Force*)

Jimmy Doolittle won the Thompson Trophy Race in 1932 flying a borrowed *Gee Bee* R-1. He attained an average speed of 252.686 mph to win the trophy and the $4,500 prize money. He is shown here with Charles E. Thompson, donor of the trophy, and Mrs. Thompson. (*Photo courtesy of U.S. Air Force*)

Still undaunted, Doolittle asked to try a third time and again his request was granted. Making sure that the barograph was installed properly and that the officials were ready, he took off and made six passes down the course, instead of the required four. His best time for one of the runs was an ear-shattering 306.99 miles per hour. When he taxied in afterward, his windshield completely covered with oil, the scrappy pilot learned that he had broken the landplane speed record by a healthy eighteen miles per hour this time. And this time the record was official. His average speed of 296.287 miles per hour for all the runs also gave him a prize of $1,575 for being the fastest qualifier.

Two days after setting this record, Doolittle was ready for the Thompson Race. His competitors were the fastest men in the world: Colonel Roscoe Turner, James Wedell, Jimmy Haizlip, William Ong, Ray Moore, Les Bowen, Robert Hall, and Lee Gehlmach, to mention a few.

As if to prove that it was a difficult plane to deal with, Doolittle's *Gee Bee* acted as if it didn't want to race any more. As Doolittle began to taxi it up to the starting line, the engine backfired, the fuel in the carburetor caught fire, and the engine started to blaze. Doolittle quickly shut the engine down, leaped out and helped the ground crew put out the fire. Fortunately, a thorough inspection showed no damage. Doolittle quickly started it up again and taxied out to the line, where seven other planes were purring noisily.

Doolittle was second off the ground in the timed departure sequence and quickly passed the first man off. Although every other pilot tried to catch up, it was Doolittle's race from then on. He passed every pilot in the field at least once and when the race was over, Jimmy pocketed $4,500 as the winner. His speed averaged out to 252.686 mph for the 100-mile course around the race pylons.

When the last race was over, Jimmy hopped into the borrowed *Gee Bee* and flew it back to Springfield, Massachusetts. "I landed it," he said, "taxied up to the line and gratefully got out of the airplane. That was my farewell to the *Gee Bee*."

The race in the *Gee Bee* had a profound effect on Doolittle. When he got out of the speedy racer for the last time, he wondered what the future of air racing should be. The speed he had attained in the "flying death trap" would be beaten by others in later years, but he wondered if the races were really making the contribution to aviation that they should. Many men had died trying to compete against the clock and their fellow pilots. Most of the deaths could be attributed to failure of either the men or their machines to stay within their respective limitations. Doolittle made extensive preparations before each flight—checking his planes over thoroughly on the ground, then in the air. He conditioned himself physically for whatever type of flight he was to undertake by exercise and practice far in advance of the event. He had survived more than fifteen years of flying in the trial-and-error days because he was not the daredevil that the press said he was—but because he was a perfectionist and put safety above all else in his thinking and planning.

Now that aviation had reached the threshold of maturity, Jimmy felt that the time had come for those truly interested in aviation progress to examine the role of air races. By 1932, they had served a useful purpose by focusing public attention on flying but the price in planes and men had been high. Wasn't it time now to make airplanes useful to all men by encouraging their use in bringing the world closer together? Shouldn't the emphasis turn to making aviation serve world commerce, rather than to continue strictly as a sport? Why not encourage the commercial aspects and potentials of aviation, rather than exploit speed just for the sake of attaining records?

A few weeks after the Thompson Race, Jimmy made a decision. He announced that he was through with air racing. "We've learned a lot about engines and airplanes through racing," he said. "But it has been at great cost in lives and equipment. I think the time has come to give attention to safety and reliability. Commercial and military aviation must be developed so that we become strong commercially and have the best aerial fighting force in the world."

Many people did not believe that Doolittle really would retire

The Curtiss *Hawk* was one of Doolittle's favorite airplanes. He is shown here beside the speedy fighter which he demonstrated for the manufacturer in many foreign countries while on leave from the Army Air Corps. (*Photo courtesy of the National Archives*)

from racing, but he never rounded a pylon again. Instead, he devoted his time to selling Shell aviation products, the most important of which was gasoline.

In the early thirties, most aircraft engines used 91-octane gasoline. Although larger engines could be designed, their increased compression required a higher octane rating for smoother burning and decreased detonation. Jimmy pushed for the development of 100-octane gasoline by the Shell chemists. His argument was based on plans for "super planes" being developed at Wright Field by the Army Air Corps. He was "in the know" because he had kept his army contacts alive and had been told that engines of greater horsepower were needed which would, in turn, create a demand for a higher octane rating gasoline.

Shell officials had to be convinced. Although they had an aviation division, aviation products were not their chief money makers. They had specialized in 91-octane gasoline because that was the rating demanded by the airline operators and the military services. Doolittle's reply was: "No one else is doing anything about the demand that is sure to develop. Shell should be ready to meet that demand when it comes. We'll be ahead of the game because nobody else is doing anything about it."

Jimmy convinced his superiors at Shell and petroleum engineers began to design expensive new facilities. It was a wise decision because, as Doolittle predicted, the larger engines were soon built and Shell was able to supply the burgeoning demand.

As the country drifted into the greatest economic depression it had ever known, American manufacturers looked abroad for business. Curtiss-Wright again asked Shell to lend Doolittle to them for a round-the-world tour. He was asked to demonstrate the Curtiss *Hawk* fighter plane which, of course, used Shell products. Shell agreed and early in 1933 Jimmy and Jo Doolittle boarded a ship for the Far East. The five-month itinerary carried them to the Philippines, the Dutch East Indies, China, Japan, India, and Europe. At each stop, Jimmy visited commercial and military facilities and put on his usual menu of acrobatic maneuvers that left the crowds agape. His fame had preceded him and people who wondered if he was as good as the many stories said he was were firmly convinced when they saw him in action. Just as he had on his two earlier tours of South America and Europe, Jimmy proved to be the best salesman for aviation products and planes that Shell and Curtiss-Wright had ever sent forth.

While this tour was a delightful experience for the Doolittles, it also proved to be an educational experience for Jimmy. In the many hours of discussion with the pilots and military leaders of the countries he visited, he obtained an unusual insight into their thinking and planning. He was disturbed by what he saw— disturbed because some countries that were considered backward and nonprogressive by most Americans were building air forces of substantial numbers of planes and pilots. He was particularly disturbed by what he saw in Japan and Germany. In these countries much emphasis was being placed on commercial airline expansion and pilot training, which would be of great benefit if a country's leaders decided to switch to military operations.

After his return from this trip, Jimmy decided that the time had come to speak out about what he had seen and heard. The United States was falling behind in aviation progress, especially in military aviation. He began to speak at every opportunity and his views were accepted because of the reputation he had established as a pilot and scientist. Now thirty-seven years old, he felt that his role should be that of a spokesman for American air power—a responsible spokesman who would present the facts without coloring them with emotional appeals or shocking statements. An unusual opportunity came in 1934 when President Franklin Delano Roosevelt asked the Air Corps to fly the mail.

Congress had passed an act in 1925 "to encourage commercial aviation and to authorize the Postmaster General to contract for airmail service." In the years between 1918 and 1925, the Post Office Department had operated the nation's airmail itself. But the 1925 bill, called the Kelly Act, took the government out of the airmail business and authorized the carrying of mail on a contract basis by privately-owned companies. This marked the real beginning of the commercial airlines.

In a very short time, a number of airlines were operating over established routes across the country. Only mail was transported at first and pilots considered passengers a nuisance. In fact, in the first few years few airmail planes had any seats installed. However, as the planes became more reliable, passengers were carried in ever larger numbers. Later, by altering the basis of payment from weight alone to the volume of space available for mail, Congress encouraged the airlines to buy larger planes that could haul both passengers and mail.

When airmail contracts expired, the postmaster general consistently favored those lines with the strongest financial backing. The smaller lines that refused to merge with larger ones and could not survive without the mail contracts were doomed. Their resentment and the allegation of scandal led to a congressional investigation. To bring the matter to a head, President Roosevelt cancelled all airmail contracts in February 1934.

In order to keep airmail service going, the Army Air Corps was asked to carry on. In the "can do" spirit that has become a tradition with the nation's flying service, Major General Benjamin D. Foulois, Chief of the Air Corps, accepted the assignment. However, he knew that the pursuit, bombing, training, and observation planes were poorly equipped to fly scheduled runs in all kinds of weather. Only a handful of army test planes had blind flying instruments installed and only about a dozen military pilots had any real experience in weather flying.

Foulois knew that he was taking on a difficult and hazardous task. But he treated the requirement as a peacetime test "under conditions simulating war conditions, in order to discover every possible peacetime weakness in organization, equipment and training. . . ."

In the ensuing weeks, there were a number of crashes, although only four fatalities occurred on actual mail flights. Six other men had died in mail training or ferrying flights.

The public uproar that resulted from the crashes caused the President to authorize new commercial contacts and the Air Corps went back to its Depression-ridden status with obsolete planes and inadequate funds for training pilots and crews. A full investigation of the Air Corps was ordered and a committee, headed by Newton D. Baker, former secretary of war during World War I, was appointed to study not only the "adequacy and efficiency" of Air Corps technical flying equipment and training but all phases of military operations.

In addition to several army officers, including General Foulois, three pilots were asked to serve: Clarence Chamberlain, Charles A. Lindbergh, and Jimmy Doolittle. Lindbergh declined, but the other two accepted the opportunity to contribute their thoughts on the future of military aviation.

During 25 days of testimony recorded on 4,300 pages of transcript, the committee heard 105 witnesses, including generals, admirals, airline pilots, and specialists in engines, instruments, blind flying, and meteorology.

Although 536 Air Corps officers had filed letters in support of the nation's principal air arm, the final report reflected the thinking of those on the committee who did not visualize the potential of the airplane as a military weapon. The report said:

> . . . the limitations of the airplane show that the ideas that aviation, acting alone, can control the sea lanes, or defend the coast, or produce decisive results . . . are all visionary as is the idea that a very large and independent air force is necessary to defend our country against air attack." The committee report then noted that "the fear that has been cultivated in this country by various zealots that American aviation is inferior to that of the rest of the world is, as a whole, unfounded. The public, ever fearful for the national security, as well as receptive to the idea of centralization as a means of securing economy and efficiency, gives credence to comparative statements of strength, powers and limitations of air forces which are often at variance with fact.

The committee concluded by condemning the air officers who sought a separate budget, a separate promotion list, and freedom from the bias of the General Staff, and accused them of "continuing agitation" and disturbing "harmonious development and improvement."

The final report was concurred in by all the members except

one. In the interest of harmony, even General Foulois decided to sign. As he told the author, "I know it was a compromise but it contained some concessions that meant a step forward for the Air Corps and that was better than no step at all."

The lone dissenter, who asked permission to present a minority statement, was Jimmy Doolittle. After Foulois read it, he wished he had joined him in signing it. The statement said:

I believe in aviation—both civil and military. I believe that the future security of our Nation is dependent upon an adequate air force. This is true at the present time and will become increasingly important as the science of aviation advances and the airplane lends itself more and more to the art of warfare. I am convinced that the required air force can be more rapidly organized, equipped and trained if it is completely separated from the Army and developed as an entirely separate arm. If complete separation is not the desire of the committee, I recommend an air force as a part of the Army but with a separate budget, a separate promotion list and removed from the control of the General Staff. These are my sincere convictions. Failing either, I feel that the Air Corps should be developed and expanded under the direction of the General Staff as recommended above.

It was to be thirteen years before the Doolittle recommendation would be accepted and carried out. Unfortunately, it would take another world war to prove conclusively that a strong air force could bring about decisive results in modern warfare.

Jimmy continued to speak his mind in public in the years following. In a speech after the last meeting of the Baker Committee, he warned that the U.S. Army Air Corps was extremely "weak in modern military aircraft and trained military pilots." Later, speaking before the National Safety Congress, he stunned air racing enthusiasts by declaring: "Air racing as a spectacle has outlived its usefulness."

He added: "Air racing originally did promote safety in aviation through testing of materials used in construction of planes and engines, and probably still does so. But lately, it appears that the value received is not commensurate with the personal risk involved."

The type of air racing that Doolittle was denouncing as having served its purpose was the pylon-shaving, dangerously low altitude racing of high performance planes that skirted the thin edge of aerodynamic stability. At speeds above three hundred miles per hour, it seemed that there was no margin for pilot or mechanical maintenance error and the inevitable penalty was mangled wreckage and death. The result could only slow down the acceptance of aviation by the public.

What was needed, in Doolittle's view, was a new kind of racing—against the clock and in passenger/cargo planes. This kind of flying would prove that people and goods could go faster from point to point. It was this rationale which caused Jimmy to plan a race from Burbank to New York in an eight-passenger single-engine *Vultee*.

Characteristically, Jimmy planned every detail of his flight carefully. He tested the plane thoroughly and asked Jo if she would like to come along as a passenger. He also invited Robert Adamson, a Shell Oil Company official, to accompany them.

"What is it this time, Jim?" Mrs. Doolittle asked. "Whose record are we going to beat?"

"Eddie Rickenbacker's," Jimmy answered, confidently. "He's got the coast-to-coast record for passenger transport planes of 12 hours and 3 minutes. We can lower that."

"Sure we can," Jo said, smiling. She knew full well that if her husband had set his mind to this task, she had only to be ready when he said it was time to go.

Doolittle chose mid-January as the time for the attempt. High-level winds, sometimes more than one hundred miles per hour, came roaring out of the west to help a plane along. These are now called "jet streams," which commercial airliners try to ride whenever they can to reduce trip times and save fuel.

The route Jimmy chose to fly was direct, rather than the airways used by the airliners, which tended to zigzag from city to city. Equipped with two-way radio and oxygen equipment, his scheme was to take the shortest route and go above the weather if he could.

On the evening of January 14, 1935, Jimmy loaded Jo and Robert Adamson into passenger seats and fired up the 735-horsepower Wright Cyclone engine. It was already dark as the *Vultee* took off, climbed to 15,000 feet, and leveled off. Clouds were heavy and did not dissipate as Jimmy headed the plane eastward.

Although weather reports had indicated that he should run out of the clouds over northern Arizona, he was still flying on instruments when his elapsed time was up. Ice began to form on the wings and the airspeed indicator showed a decrease in airspeed. The radio antenna, encrusted with ice, caused the radio to go dead. The only thing to do was to steer south into warmer air. He did and although the ice finally melted and broke off, Jimmy was still on instruments and it was a long time until morning light might give him a clue to his position.

Hour after long night hour, the *Vultee* bored eastward. Although Jimmy didn't know it, the wind had changed from west to northwest and the *Vultee* was being blown far south of its intended course. As the first light of dawn enabled Jimmy to see outside the craft, he found that the clouds were breaking up. The sun came through and he saw landmarks that he recognized. Turning to his passengers, he pointed downward and yelled, "Richmond!"

Although he was far south of his original course and dead tired from wrestling the *Vultee* all night long on instruments, he made a quick calculation and figured that he could still break the Rickenbacker record. Turning northward and gradually descending to gain additional speed, he set the *Vultee* down at Floyd Bennett Airport.

The flight had been made in 11 hours, 59 minutes—ten seconds short of beating the old record by a full five minutes. When he was interviewed by the press, Doolittle, dog-tired and not at all pleased with his performance, said, "I got off course. I should have been here an hour and a half sooner."

Very few people understood what it meant for a pilot to fly

instruments at night and attempt to cross the country with no navigational aids. Many people hailed the trip as just another stunt but a few recognized the flight's real significance for air transportation. If a single-engine passenger plane could make the nonstop trip in less than half a day without any difficulty, aviation had indeed come a long way.

11. Back in Uniform

THE YEARS AFTER THE 1935 transcontinental record flight were busy ones for the fast-moving Doolittle. He gave many talks and lectures about aviation subjects and flew all over the country to lend his knowledge and experience to aircraft manufacturers, aeronautical scientists, and the military services. He remained active in the Air Corps Reserve and served his annual two-week active duty tours as a major.

Jimmy's status as a respected scientist with an insatiable curiosity kept him abreast of every important aviation development in the country. He received many awards and honors for his past accomplishments during the five-year period, 1935-1940. He was named president of the Institute of Aeronautical Sciences, an honor reserved for those who have made genuine contributions to aviation progress.

But disturbing things were happening in the world during this period. A man named Adolf Hitler had taken over the government of Germany. A bloody civil war had been fought in Spain and Russia, and Germany had sent pilots and planes to fight on opposing sides. Europe was like a stick of dynamite whose fuse had already been lit. It was just a matter of time before it went off.

Jimmy made two more trips to Europe. In 1937, he stayed at the apartment of Ernst Udet, famous World War I ace who had flown at the Cleveland Air Races and was considered Germany's top pilot. The friendship between the two resulted in Jimmy seeing far more evidence of Germany's aviation progress than other visitors. The nation that was not supposed to have an air force was building hundreds of training planes, fighters, and bombers. On March 6, 1935, Hitler had repudiated all treaties that had placed limitations on German armaments and created the Luftwaffe. The German Fuehrer had thereby thumbed his nose at the Allies who had won World War I and was getting away with it.

Jimmy rushed home from this trip and did all he could to spur American civilian and military officials into action to produce better planes and equipment. He continued his push for industry-wide development of 100-octane gasoline to meet the technological threat to American aviation supremacy he had seen in Europe.

But Americans were not ready to think of war. They were just pulling out of a serious economic depression with a new President. Government funds were needed to carry out the many "pump priming" experiments that were characteristic of the New Deal. "Let the Europeans fight their own wars," most Americans said. "We've got problems of our own to solve."

Jimmy returned to Germany in the spring of 1939. By this time, Hitler had annexed Austria and taken over Czechoslovakia. Airplanes and armaments he had seen two years before had now multiplied. The planes that were on the drawing boards when he had been there two years before were now on the flying line. Hundreds of pilots had been trained and were fired up with the Hitlerite war preachings. The sight of thousands of uniformed youths shouting "Down with the Jews! Down with the Catholics! Heil Hitler!" was frighteningly ominous. There was absolutely no doubt in Doolittle's mind that all of Europe would soon be ablaze in a new war that could easily turn into another world war because of the alignment of Germany, Italy, and Japan in what was called the Axis.

Jimmy left Germany and flew to London, where he reported to the American air attaché assigned to the U.S. Embassy. The attaché did not share Doolittle's concern and suggested he put his observations down in writing so they could be sent to the War Department. The naval attaché, who had heard of the trip, contacted Jimmy, patiently made notes, thanked him, and bade him a pleasant boat trip back to the States. It was clear that neither man was going to do more than make a routine report that would be filed and forgotten.

If these people won't listen, Doolittle told himself, he would see General Henry H. "Hap" Arnold, his former commanding officer in World War I, who had risen to become Chief of the Air Corps.

In Washington, Arnold was glad to see Doolittle and was grateful for the information his former subordinate passed on to him. The two talked for a long time and finally, Doolittle said quietly, "Hap, there's going to be a big war soon and I want to be in on it."

"How do you mean?" Arnold queried.

"I want to come back on active duty," Doolittle answered.

Arnold was surprised and pleased that the man who had become so famous by winning all the important aviation trophies and had set so many records would volunteer to go back in uniform at a major's pay. "Jim, I'd like to have you back but I'm forbidden by Congress to call anyone to active duty above the rank of captain until next July first."

"I'll wait," Jimmy said.

At dawn, September 1, 1939, war did indeed come to Europe as 1,400 Luftwaffe planes bombed and strafed a stunned Poland. With contemptuous ease, the *blitzkrieg* rolled on until the 36,000 square miles of Poland was annexed to Germany. On September 3, Great Britain declared war on Germany and France reluctantly followed suit.

A week later President Roosevelt declared a state of national emergency and decreed that the United States was to become "the arsenal of democracy." At that time, the United States began to build its air power by providing orders that enabled the aviation industry to expand factory facilities and tool up for mass production. The air components of the army and navy, under-equipped and under-manned for many years, were now faced with the seemingly impossible task of defending a continent against attack and preparing for what now appeared to be a second world war.

On May 16, 1940, President Roosevelt appeared before Congress to make a significant speech. Six days before, the Netherlands, Belgium, and France had been "blitzed" and the Allies faced grave danger of annihilation. "These are ominous days," he said, "days whose swift and shocking developments force every neutral nation to look to its defenses."

Commenting on "the amazing progress in the design of planes and engines," he called for a program that would produce "at least 50,000 planes a year."

France surrendered to the Nazis on June 22, 1940. Now only Great Britain alone remained at war with Germany. It was at this critical point in history that Jimmy Doolittle returned to extended active duty.

The transition back to uniform was not difficult for Doolittle, although he detected a touch of jealousy among his contemporaries who had stayed on active duty through the lean Depression years. Some of them thought Doolittle had left the service "to feather his nest" and become rich. Some resented the fact that he had never served as a captain and was recalled to duty as a major, thus "outranking" many of those he had served with in the 1920s. But Doolittle had no time to worry about what others thought of his motivations.

On July 1, 1940, orders were issued assigning him to Indianapolis, Indiana, for duty as assistant district supervisor of the Central Air Corps Procurement District. Four months later, he was transferred to Detroit.

These assignments were made by General Arnold personally and were not an attempt to give Doolittle an easy job. The President's plans to make the United States the arsenal of democracy meant that American industry had to be converted from peacetime goods to implements of war. Retooling and reorganizing to turn out new and unfamiliar products was a mammoth and nearly impossible job.

Arnold, who was a genius at picking the right man for a job, knew that Doolittle was one of the few men in the country who had the necessary engineering and technical background to deal with complex industrial problems. Converting the automobile industry to mass production of airplanes and parts was one of the most difficult tasks in American industrial history. By the time of the "day of infamy"—December 7, 1941—the entire automotive industry had agreed to their "terminal quotas" of cars for the duration of the war that had been thrust upon the nation by the bombing of Pearl Harbor. Doolittle's wise counsel and great tact had done much to make the conversion to war production as smooth as possible.

The day before Christmas 1941, Arnold telephoned Doolittle in Detroit and asked him to come to Washington to be on his staff. "I've got to be sure that we get the flying equipment we need in the months to come and that it can do the job when we get it," Arnold said. "I think you can help."

Doolittle understood perfectly and immediately left for the nation's capital. In peacetime, because of budgetary restrictions, the Air Corps had to be more interested in aircraft performance than in how the various planes might be employed in combat. In wartime, planes had to do more than fly high and fast. They had to be capable of carrying the fight to the enemy's homeland.

Upon arrival in Washington, Arnold assigned Doolittle the job of troubleshooter. The role appealed to Doolittle provided he didn't have to "fly a desk" for the duration. He had missed one war and he didn't want to miss another.

The first task given Doolittle by Arnold was "the B-26 problem." Doolittle recalled:

The B-26 *Marauder* was an unforgiving airplane and it was killing pilots because it never gave them a chance to make mistakes. General Arnold wanted me to check into the problem and recommend whether it should be continued to be built or not. I checked it over, flew it and liked it. There wasn't anything about its flying characteristics that good piloting skill couldn't overcome. I recommended that it continue to be built and it was.

General Arnold confirmed this in his memoirs:

> Our new pilots were afraid of the B-26 and we had one accident after another. Seemingly, all that was necessary was for one engine to go sour on a B-26 in flight, and it would crash.
>
> At the time the B-26 trouble was at its height, I called Doolittle to my office, told him I would like to have him go out, take a B-26, fly it under any and all conditions, and then go down to the B-26 outfit, take command, and show those boys that flying this ship was no different from flying any other. Doolittle did this, and before he left the outfit he had the boys flying the B-26 on one engine, making landings, and taking off with one engine, just as easily as they had formerly done with two.*

When this task was nearing completion, Arnold called Doolittle in and asked, "Jim, what airplane have we got that will get off in five hundred feet with a two thousand pound bomb load and fly two thousand miles?"

Doolittle pondered the question. The Air Force had planes that could take off within five hundred feet but none that could do that and fly a ton of bombs two thousand miles. However, if properly modified, maybe the B-18, B-23, or the B-25 could do it. The B-26 was definitely out because it needed much more runway to get airborne.

"General, I'll need a little time to give you an answer."

"O.K., Jim," Arnold said, "but keep this quiet and let me know as soon as you can."

The next day, Doolittle had the answer. "It narrows down to the B-23 or the B-25, but either one will have to have gas added."

"One thing I should have mentioned," Arnold said. "The plane must take off from a narrow area not over 75 feet wide."

"Then the B-25 is the answer," Jimmy said. "The B-23's wing-

---

* Arnold, Henry H., *Global Mission*, p. 259. New York: Harper and Brothers, 1949.

span would make it a close call. Now, what's behind the question?"

Arnold quickly passed on an idea that had been given to him by Adm. Ernest J. King, Chief of Naval Operations. Essentially, the idea was a simple one in concept. The navy would load a few of the army's medium bombers on a carrier and take them within striking distance of Japan. Army pilots would take off, bomb military targets in Japan, and fly to safety in China. Doolittle had, unknowingly, decided which bomber would be used. The basic question unanswered was whether the land-based, twin-engine B-25 *Mitchell* bomber could take off within the short length of a carrier's deck.

Doolittle developed an enthusiasm for the idea immediately. "Jim," Arnold said, "I need someone to take this project over, get the planes modified and train the crews."

"And I know where you can get that someone," Doolittle replied. He immediately plunged into planning for what was destined to become a classic air operation in military history.

12. "I Don't Deserve
the Big Medal!"

THE STORY OF THE Doolittle raid really begins on January 4, 1942, when the basic concept of launching land-based army bombers from the deck of a navy carrier was born in the fertile brain of General Arnold. During conferences with the British between December 24, 1941, and January 14, 1942, Arnold and the other Combined Chiefs met with President Roosevelt and Prime Minister Winston Churchill in the White House. One of the subjects of great concern was the unsettled French situation in North Africa. Adm. Ernest J. King, Chief of Naval Operations, recommended that a naval force transport land and air forces to the North Africa centered around three carriers, two of which would transport army fighters and bombers to be off-loaded by cranes when the ships could move into the harbors.

"Hap" Arnold was disturbed by these arrangements. His planes would be sitting ducks until they could be moved to an airfield, and there was no reliable estimate as to how much resistance would be encountered during the landing operations. He went back to his office and transcribed his notes of that day's meeting. He wrote: "We will have to try bomber takeoffs from carriers. It has never been done before but we must try [it] out and check on how long it takes."

While Arnold's staff was thinking about this idea, Capt. Francis L. Low, a submariner on Admiral King's staff, had a flash of what he later called "fortuitous association." King had urged all of his staff members to think of some way that the attack on Pearl Harbor could be avenged and Low was doing just that. On a flight to Norfolk, Virginia, he had noticed some army twin-engine bombers (he didn't know what type) making simulated bombing passes at the outline of a carrier painted on an airfield. This picture stimulated a question in his mind. Could army bombers take off from a carrier's deck? If so, could a navy carrier get them near enough to Japan so that they could bomb Tokyo and escape to China? He didn't know the answers, but he passed the idea along to Capt. Donald B. "Wu" Duncan, King's air officer.

At the admiral's direction, Duncan studied the problem for five days and concluded that the Army Air Force's B-25, if properly modified, could carry 2,000 pounds of bombs and fly a 2,000-mile mission. King referred Duncan to "Hap" Arnold, who thanked Duncan for his work and immediately sent down the hall for Jimmy Doolittle.

It took Doolittle only a few hours to verify Duncan's figures. When he did, Arnold immediately assigned him the task of planning and preparing the Army Air Force's part of the mission. King assigned Duncan as project officer for the navy. Both men, perfectionists and skilled persuaders, went their separate ways to carry out the basic plan, which was a model of simplicity yet had to be carried out with the greatest secrecy.

The navy would transport sixteen B-25 bombers to about 450 miles off the coast of Japan and launch them. The B-25s would proceed to bomb military targets in Japan and fly to safe havens in China.

Once the type of plane had been decided, the decision as to which units would furnish planes and men was easy. The B-25 Mitchell was just entering the AAF operational inventory and the only units with any experience with it were the three squadrons of the Seventeenth Bomb Group—the Thirty-fourth, Thirty-seventh, and Ninety-fifth—and the Eighty-ninth Reconnaissance Squadron, co-located with the Seventeenth at Pendleton, Oregon. Scheduled to move to Columbia, South Carolina, in February, almost every crew member in the four squadrons had already flown anti-submarine missions off the Oregon-Washington coast. One plane, piloted by Lt. Everett W. "Brick" Holstrom (now a brigadier general), had sunk the first Japanese submarine destroyed off the United States.

While the men and planes were en route to South Carolina, Doolittle contacted the unit commanders and asked for volunteers "for an extremely hazardous mission." Every man who heard of the call immediately volunteered, including the four squadron commanders. Doolittle chose Maj. (later Brig. Gen.) John A. Hilger as his second-in-command and gave him the task of choosing the required air and ground crews and getting them to Eglin Field, Florida, where they would get the planes modified and themselves trained for a mission that could not be revealed to them. Twenty-four crews would be chosen, trained, and transported although only sixteen planes were to go aboard the carrier. The eight extra crews would provide replacements but also prevent any of the disappointed men from divulging any information or speculating on where their buddies had gone. Each crew would consist of five men—pilot, copilot, bombardier, navigator, and mechanic-gunner.

While the men were being chosen and some of the planes were being modified with extra gas tanks, a seemingly unrelated mission was taking place at Norfolk. There the navy's newest aircraft carrier, *Hornet,* was made ready for a one-day trip off the East Coast. Two B-25s were hoisted aboard and lashed down. The *Hornet* sailed out of sight of land and the B-25s were made ready for flight. "Wu" Duncan climbed up on the bridge to watch. The question uppermost in his mind was whether a B-25 could take off from the *Hornet's* deck. When the pilots, Army Air Forces Lts. John E. Fitzgerald and James F. McCarthy, were briefed, they wondered, too. There was less than 450 feet of usable deck space for them. However, they had been practicing short-field takeoffs on land for about two weeks and had gotten off in almost that short a distance. They hoped that the speed of the carrier and the speed of the wind would make up the difference.

Fitzgerald, who already had four hundred hours in the Mitchell, was relieved when he saw that the airspeed indicator in his plane registered forty-five miles an hour just sitting on the deck. The wind over the deck plus the speed of the carrier meant that only about twenty-five miles an hour acceleration had to be provided by the plane's engines to become airborne. Fitzgerald, unaware of the significance of his mission, describes the first carrier takeoff ever made by an Army Air Forces medium bomber:

> When I got the "go" signal, I let the brakes off and was almost immediately airborne—well ahead of my estimate. One thing that worried me, though, was the projection of the island structure out over the flight deck on which the skipper stood so he could have a clear view of the deck operations. The wing of my plane rose so rapidly that I thought we were going to strike this projection. I pushed the control column forward and the wing just barely passed underneath. I climbed and circled back to watch Lieutenant McCarthy take off.

McCarthy also made it safely off and both planes returned to Norfolk. Duncan, satisfied now that a combat-laden B-25 could make a carrier takeoff, ordered a skilled flying instructor, Lt. Henry L. Miller (now a rear admiral) from Pensacola, to Eglin to teach the army pilots the proper techniques. Although almost all of the pilots guessed that their mission had something to do with carrier operations, none of them openly speculated about it, because Doolittle had warned them not to discuss their speculations even among themselves.

Although Miller had never seen a B-25 before, he taught all the pilots the strange (for them) techniques for getting a heavily loaded plane off the runway in a distance about the length of a football field. They didn't know it then but before they finished Miller's course they would be able to take off from 350 feet in a

40-knot wind with the plane loaded to 31,000 pounds—2,000 pounds over its designed maximum load.

Since the mission required absolute radio silence and weight was a problem, the 230-pound liaison radio set was removed, along with other nonessential items. To prevent the possible loss of the secret Norden bombsight, and since it was found to be inaccurate at the low levels intended for the mission, Capt. Ross Greening designed a simple aluminum "Mark Twain" bombsight in the Eglin shops at a cost of twenty cents. It proved to be highly accurate and was installed and used in all of the aircraft.

The two gun turrets installed in the top and bottom of the rear fuselage proved to be a worrisome problem. The bottom turret proved so difficult to operate that Doolittle ordered it taken out of all planes and replaced by a sixty-gallon fuel tank. He also directed that two broomsticks be painted black and installed in the tail cone of each plane to simulate twin .50-caliber machine guns. It was hoped that an enemy fighter pilot would avoid tail-end passes in favor of another direction, where the top gunner or nose gunner could blast him.

In spite of leaky gas tanks and continual problems with the top gun turret, the "Special B-25 Project" was ordered to proceed to the West Coast during the last week of March. On April 1, the sixteen B-25s were hoisted aboard the *Hornet* at Alameda; the next morning eight ships sailed under the Golden Gate Bridge and headed west. When he was out of sight of land, Capt. Marc A. Mitscher, commander of Task Force 16.2, blinkered his ships: THIS FORCE IS HEADED FOR TOKYO. When the announcement was made on each ship's intercom, all hands cheered mightily.

Below decks, Doolittle called his men together and gave them all the essential details of their mission: the nature of the targets to be hit, topographical data, escape and evasion information, and the expected defenses around the five target cities of Tokyo, Yokohama, Nagoya, Osaka, and Kobe. After dropping their bombs, they would all head south, then west across the China Sea to five fields in China where they would refuel and then proceed to Chungking. Doolittle then allowed the sixteen crews to select their targets.

For the next two weeks, the entire Doolittle contingent worked on their planes, sharpened their gunnery by firing at target kites, listened to first aid lectures by Lt. Thomas R. White, a physician who volunteered to go on the raid as a gunner, and worried about their individual chances for survival. The closer they got to the takeoff day (scheduled for April 19), the more the tension could be felt aboard the *Hornet.*

There was good reason for concern, although not a single man in the task force knew it. On April 10, Japanese radio intelligence officers had intercepted "conversations" between the Mitscher force and the eight-ship force of Adm. William F. Halsey which was scheduled to join up at the 180th meridian. The enemy calculated that there was a large task force headed toward Japan built around two or three carriers which should arrive within 650 miles of Japan by April 14. As a result, defensive air and ground forces were positioned around Tokyo and naval units were ordered to proceed to a general interception area. A line of fifty picket ships positioned about 650 miles out from the Japanese coast was alerted and navy patrol bombers were put on twenty-four-hour search duty.

Although the enemy ability to intercept messages and deduce valuable information from them was exceptional, they made an error in their basic assumptions. They assumed that the Americans were going to pay an avenging call on Tokyo by steaming within carrier plane striking distance, just as the Japanese had done at Pearl Harbor. This would mean that the Americans would have to launch their planes about two hundred to three hundred miles out. They had no idea that there were army bombers lashed to the deck of one of the carriers; even if they had known it, they would never have believed that those bombers were to be launched from that deck. As one Japanese intelligence officer admitted after the war, "We would have thought anything like that absolutely impossible."

On the afternoon of April 15, the carriers and cruisers in the task force were refueled. The oilers and destroyers withdrew to await the return of the larger ships after the B-25s were loaded with bombs; armament crews loaded the twin fifties in the top turret and the single .30-caliber gun in the nose; mechanics made last-minute engine adjustments and continued to try to stop the gas leaks which plagued all the planes. Doolittle gave his men a final briefing and warned them once more about hitting only assigned military targets.

"Whatever you do," he told them, "don't go after the Imperial Palace. It's not worth an oil refinery, a plane factory or a steel mill, so leave it alone."

As darkness came on the evening of the seventeenth, the tension on board the *Hornet* increased. Although it had been originally planned to launch the B-25s on April 19, the launching force would now arrive at the takeoff point a whole day early. This fact was not known in Washington or Chungking. As later events were to prove, this unannounced change—which the navy has never explained—would make a big difference in the outcome of the mission.

Radar operators aboard the aircraft carrier *Enterprise* picked up a blip on their screen at 3:05 A.M. and Halsey immediately ordered the force to turn northward. When the blip faded the six ships turned westward again. At dawn, Halsey launched search planes from the "Big E" and a combat air patrol above the two carriers. The weather slowly worsened with each passing minute and the *Hornet* began to buck and toss as green water smashed over the bow and down the deck.

At 5:58 A.M. Lt. O. B. Wiseman, flying an SBD scout plane, dropped a message on the *Hornet's* deck saying that he had spotted an enemy surface ship forty-two miles from the task force. He added a cryptic note: "Believe seen by enemy."

The moment of decision had come. Halsey immediately ordered the cruiser *Nashville* to sink the enemy vessel. At exactly 8 A.M., he blinked a message to Mitscher aboard the *Hornet:*

LAUNCH PLANES X TO COL DOOLITTLE
AND GALLANT COMMAND
GOOD LUCK AND GOD BLESS YOU

Jimmy Doolittle was on the *Hornet's* bridge when the message was given to Mitscher. He hurriedly shook hands and leaped down the ladder to his cabin, shouting to everyone he saw, "Okay, fellas, this is it! Let's go!" At the same time the blood-chilling klaxon horn sounded and Mitscher's voice came over the loudspeaker: "Army pilots, man your planes!"

The weather had gone from bad to worse and the carrier's deck was rolling and pitching. The Doolittle crews had difficulty getting to their planes with their bags and equipment as the slippery deck seesawed under them.

On signal, Doolittle started his engines and warmed them up. When his instruments were in the green, he gave a thumbs-up signal to the launching officer, Lt. Edgar G. Osborne. Osborne raised his checkered flag and began to swing it in a circle over his head as a signal for Doolittle to ease the throttles forward. Osborne swung the flag in faster and faster circles. At the precise instant the deck was beginning an upward movement, the chocks were pulled from under Mitchell's wheels and Osborne chopped the flag down. Doolittle released the brakes and the B-25 inched forward. It seemed to waddle at first and then lunged slowly into the gale that swept down the deck. Within a few yards and just as the *Hornet's* bow reached the peak of a wave, the wheels parted from the deck and Doolittle was airborne with plenty of deck space to spare. He climbed steeply, leveled off, and then came around in a tight circle. He lined up with the deck, checked his compass against the carrier's direction, and sped toward Tokyo.

While most of the pilots had no difficulty getting off, one forgot his flaps and dipped down below the deck level after clearing the deck; however, he managed to recover his speed before hitting the waves. Another plane suffered a cracked nose cone when it rammed into the tail cone of the plane ahead during the deck handling operation. But it was the last plane on the deck that had the most difficulty. Since its tail was hanging out over the end of the deck, it could not be loaded until the one ahead had moved forward. While the pilot, Lt. William G. Farrow, idled the engines, deck handlers held the nose wheel down. A sudden

The first B-25 to leave the deck of the *Hornet* was piloted by Doolittle who had the shortest deck space for the take-off run. All sixteen B-25's got off safely although none of the pilots had ever made a carrier take-off before. (*Photo courtesy of the U.S. Air Force*)

(*Left*) The day before the famous raid on Tokyo, Doolittle and his crews gathered on the deck of the USS *Hornet* for a ceremony. Medals, awarded to navy personnel between wars by the Japanese, were returned "with interest" via bombs dropped from the B-25 *Mitchells*. Doolittle is shown pinning one on the fin of a 500-pound bomb while crewmen look on. (*Photo courtesy of the U.S. Air Force*)

blast of air from the plane ahead knocked them off their feet. One of them, Seaman Robert W. Wall, slipped into Farrow's idling left propeller. There was nothing Farrow could do. The prop chewed into Wall's left arm and threw him aside. His buddies crawled to him and carried him to sick bay where his arm was amputated a short time later. Farrow's crew, slightly shaken by what they had witnessed, were jockeyed into position and took off at 9:20 A.M.—exactly one hour after Doolittle had departed.

While the sixteen planes were winging westward through rain squalls in a long ragged line, the cruiser *Nashville* had been pumping shells into the Japanese picket ship and planes from the *Enterprise* were strafing it whenever the cruiser ceased fire. The enemy craft was no match for this concentration of fire power and it finally slid beneath the waves.

As soon as the last bomber was gone, the entire American naval force reversed course. It was none too soon. Japanese patrol planes were picked up on the radar, but none came closer than thirty miles. The poor visibility and low ceilings were allies. For the next two hours, planes from both carriers flew patrol missions and engaged several other picket boats. One of them, the *Nagato Maru*, was sunk, but five survivors were picked up to become the first prisoners taken in combat by the navy in World War II.

The escaping task force steamed away at full speed for two days and two nights. During the daylight hours, patrol planes kept watch above. Although they sighted many enemy vessels, Halsey decided not to attack them as long as they did not menace the force. Two of his planes, however, had to ditch because they ran out of gas. Two men on one plane were not recovered. Other planes were severely damaged in landing accidents. In spite of these mishaps, the navy had a right to be proud of their part in the mission. The B-25s had been launched successfully and the entire task force had escaped without a scratch.

The line of B-25s plunged on toward Japan unaware of what was happening to the task force. They had other problems. Several of them dodged Japanese patrol planes and Japanese ships.

As they neared the coast, the weather improved and, one by one, they burst out of the clouds and fog into a bright, crisp spring day. Only one or two of the pilots could see the plane ahead. All of them were having difficulty with their magnetic compasses, gas leaks, and faulty top gun turrets. Navigators, unable to get fixes, were frantically trying to locate their positions on their maps as soon as the coastline showed up.

First over the coast was Doolittle. His navigator, Lt. Hank Potter, immediately spotted an identifiable landmark and told his pilot that they were north of Tokyo and should turn south. Doolittle complied and soon saw the sprawling Japanese capital ahead. Lining up with a large factory complex, his bombardier, Sgt. Fred Braemer, opened the bomb bay doors and adjusted his Mark Twain bombsight. At exactly thirty minutes past noon, he triggered off four incendiary bombs and quickly closed the doors. Doolittle felt the plane lighten. He dove for the rooftops of downtown Tokyo and sped out over Tokyo Bay on his southward escape route.

The second and third planes, piloted by Lts. Travis Hoover and Bob Gray, quickly found their targets and dropped their bombs on warehouses, a factory, a gas plant, and the Tokyo dock area. The crew of Capt. Davy Jones watched their bombs smash into a power plant and an oil tank farm. Bombs from the planes of Capt. Ed York and Lts. Ted Lawson, Dean Hallmark, Harold Watson, and Dick Joyce blasted steel mills, factories, power stations, and a gas plant.

A flight of three planes, led by Capt. Ross Greening, headed for the Yokohama dock area. Sgt. Bill Birch watched hypnotized as his bombs shattered an oil refinery and its nearby tank farm. The bombs from the planes of Lts. Bill Bower and Ed McElroy hit the dock area and Lt. Dick Knobloch, McElroy's copilot, watched as their bombs landed squarely on a merchant ship being converted into an aircraft carrier. Almost as if in slow motion, it rolled over and sank in its floating dry dock.

The tenth plane assigned to bomb Tokyo had been having trouble since takeoff. Gas tanks started leaking, the top turret refused to function, and the magnetic compass proved to be more than sixty degrees off. As a result, while the other planes were flying down Tokyo Bay toward him, Lt. Everett W. "Brick" Holstrom, coming in from the south, found himself going upstream against them. He could see the black bursts of flak over the city ahead and the fighter planes buzzing around as if confused by all the planes going in so many different directions. He had earlier given instructions to his bombardier-gunner in the nose, Cpl. Bert Jordan, to salvo all bombs if they were attacked by fighters from above. With one hand on the .30-caliber machine gun and the other on the salvo handle, Jordan watched a large group of enemy fighters circling above. When his buddy in the inoperable top turret yelled that they were being attacked he pulled the salvo handle and dropped all four bombs into Tokyo Bay. There was no reason for a bombless B-25 to take on the whole Japanese air defense force, so Holstrom wheeled the *Mitchell* around and joined the southbound stream of B-25s.

The three remaining planes had crossed the coast south of Tokyo and headed for the inland cities of Kobe and Nagoya. Maj. Jack Hilger's bombs were released on an arsenal, an army barracks area, and an aircraft factory.

Don Smith's bombardier, red-headed Lt. Howard Sessler, triggered his entire load on a steel plant. Bill Farrow, pilot of the last plane off the *Hornet,* decided to attack his secondary target in Nagoya instead of his primary in Osaka. His bombs smashed into an oil tank farm and an aircraft factory.

Few of the escaping Americans saw any of the other planes while making their escape. However, all except one proceeded southward until they cleared the island of Honshu, and then southwestward to their destinations in China. The lone exception, Capt. Ed York, found that both engines of his plane were consuming an exceptional amount of gasoline. His navigator, Lt. Nolan A. Herndon, reported that they could not possibly reach the Chinese coast. York decided to head for Vladivostok, only about six hundred miles away. While the other planes were heading for the Chinese mainland, York landed safely at a Russian airdrome. To their surprise, they were immediately placed under arrest by the Russians and their plane was confiscated.

After arriving over China at night and in bad weather because of an earlier-than-scheduled take-off, Doolittle and his crew bailed out—Doolittle for the third time in his flying career. The men are shown here with friendly Chinese soldiers who assisted them to safety. Left to right: S/Sgt. Fred A. Braemer, bombardier; S/Sgt. Paul J. Leonard, engineer-gunner; Lt. Richard E. Cole, copilot; Doolittle; Lt. Henry A. Porter, navigator. (*Photo courtesy of the U.S. Air Force*)

They spent the next thirteen months in virtual captivity because of the Russian desire to appear completely neutral in the eyes of the Japanese. The five men of this crew eventually escaped into Iran.

The fifteen planes heading toward China first ran into head-winds, then into increasingly bad weather. By the time they neared the Chinese coast, visibility was down to two miles or less in rain and the ceiling gradually lowered to less than five hundred feet. Darkness made the situation worse. Each pilot knew that he faced difficult alternatives if he could not find the destination airfields. Unknown to them all, since they were a whole day early, the Chinese warning net had caused a blackout over Free China and radio homing beacons at the fields had been turned off. Jimmy Doolittle and the pilots of ten other planes decided to bail out when their gas ran out. All the men landed with not much more than sprained ankles except Corp. Leland Faktor. His body was found the next morning by Chinese farmers. Apparently, his head had struck something on the plane as he jumped or he had waited too long to jump from the rear hatch.

Four pilots elected to crash-land their planes on or near the beach. Lt. Ted Lawson (author of the best-selling *Twenty Seconds Over Tokyo*) and his copilot, Lt. Dean Davenport, were both thrown through the windshield still strapped in their seats when their plane hit the water. Both suffered serious injuries and Lawson eventually had to have his leg amputated by "Doc" White, who had providentially caught up with him as they all evaded capture by the Japanese.

The plane piloted by Dean Hallmark also suffered bad luck in a water landing. The two enlisted men on the crew, Sgts. Bill Dieter and Donald Fitzmaurice, were seriously injured. Both died that night while trying to swim to the beach.

The other two crews that elected to crash-land were luckier. Lt. Travis Hoover made a soft wheels-up landing in a rice paddy and Lt. Don Smith landed in shallow surf only a few feet from a smooth beach. No one on these two crews were scratched.

Thirteen of the fifteen crews that had made it to the Chinese mainland eventually slipped through the Japanese lines and proceeded to Chungking. However, the surviving members of the crews of Lts. Dean Hallmark and Bill Farrow were quickly apprehended by roving Japanese patrols. In Chungking, Doolittle kept score on his men as they made their way to safety. When he learned that two crews had been captured, he offered ransom to their captors and rewards to any Chinese who could free them. He tried to persuade the ranking Chinese officer, Gen. Ku Cho-tung, to send troops to their rescue. But his efforts were in vain. There was neither enough money nor enough troops to get them back. The Japanese had eight captives upon whom they could wreak their vengeance for what their propagandists immediately branded as an "inhuman, insatiable, indiscriminate bombing attack on Japanese hospitals, schools, and homes."

Jimmy Doolittle was heartbroken when he learned that all of his planes, including the one that had landed in Russia, were lost to the Allied cause. His morale reached the lowest ebb in his life when he heard of Faktor's death and the suspected fate of the men on the Hallmark and Farrow crews. He fully expected to be court-martialed for failing to carry out his mission as he had planned. He was genuinely surprised when "Hap" Arnold wired congratulations on his promotion from lieutenant colonel, not to full colonel, but to brigadier general.

The effect on Allied morale was exactly what was needed at that most dismal time in American history. The news spread around the world that not only had Tokyo been bombed successfully by American planes launched from the *Hornet* but that the raid had been led by the incomparable Jimmy Doolittle. Headlines proclaimed: TOKYO BOMBED! DOOLITTLE DO'OD IT! It was the best news for depressed Americans that could be imagined. Not only had the Japanese capital been bombed, but it had been a surprise attack carried out exactly as the Japanese had done at Pearl Harbor—from carriers and without loss to the naval units that had made the raid possible.

While news of the daring raid spread around the globe, Doolittle was ordered home by way of India, North Africa, and South America. His instructions were to avoid the press, and as

Lt. Gen. Henry H. "Hap" Arnold, left, is seen talking with Brig. Gen. Jimmy Doolittle after the latter led his famous Tokyo Raiders against the Japanese mainland in 1942. Doolittle was promoted from grade of lieutenant colonel to one-star rank, skipping the grade of colonel. Having left the Air Corps as a first lieutenant in 1930, and being given the rank of major in the reserves, Doolittle never held rank of captain. (*Photo courtesy of the U.S. Air Force*)

far as most people knew, he was still in China. Upon arrival in Washington, he was whisked to an apartment and told to remain there until he was contacted by General Arnold. On May 20, the call came.

"Jim," Arnold said, "get your cleanest uniform on. I'm coming by to pick you up in about twenty minutes."

Doolittle dressed hurriedly. An olive-drab army sedan drove up and Doolittle bounded down the steps, saluted, and smiled broadly at his old friend now wearing the four stars of a general. Arnold grinned back and then Doolittle noticed someone else in the rear seat. It was Gen. George C. Marshall, Army Chief of Staff.

"Get in front, Jim," Arnold said. "Sorry to rush you but we haven't got much time."

"Yes, sir," Doolittle replied. He exchanged greetings with the unsmiling Marshall.

There was an uneasy silence in the car as the driver sped along Pennsylvania Avenue toward downtown Washington. When he could stand the silence no longer, Doolittle asked his superiors where they were going. Arnold grinned without answering and Marshall gave him an icy stare.

"Well," Doolittle ventured, "I think there's something going on that I don't know about. I'm not a very smart fellow and if it involves me, I think somebody had better tell me so they won't be embarrassed."

"Hap" Arnold could not contain the secret any longer. "Jimmy, we're on the way to the White House," he said. "President Roosevelt is going to give you the Medal of Honor!"

Doolittle twisted quickly in the seat with a surprised look on his face. "That's ridiculous, sir! I don't deserve the Big Medal. A commander shouldn't get a medal for failure, and I failed to carry out my mission!"

Arnold was surprised and, as Doolittle told the author later, "got mad as the devil at me." The nation and its President did not agree with the famous flier's evaluation. Upon arrival at the President's outer office, Doolittle received his second surprise when a side door opened and in stepped his wife, Jo.

After the Tokyo Raid, Doolittle was promoted to brigadier general and ordered to the White House where President Franklin D. Roosevelt presented him with the Congressional Medal of Honor in a surprise ceremony. Looking on is Lt. Gen. Henry H. "Hap" Arnold, Chief of the Army Air Forces; Mrs. Doolittle; and Gen. George C. Marshall, Army Chief of Staff. (*Photo courtesy of the U.S. Air Force*)

They could not believe their eyes. Jo had not seen her husband for over six weeks. He had told her then, "Don't worry about me. I'll be out of the country for a short while." She had no idea where he had been or what he had been doing. All she knew was that she had received a call from "Hap" Arnold who asked her to come to Washington quickly. She had been given top priority on the airlines and had arrived "looking like a carpetbagger." She could not imagine why she had been met at Washington National Airport and whisked to the White House.

Jimmy and Jo embraced while "Hap" Arnold, who had arranged the surprise reunion, chuckled in the background. A few moments later the four entered the President's office and shook hands with the man on whose shoulders rested the awesome task of bringing the nation back to its feet after five months of war which had begun the previous December 7—"a date which will live in infamy."

President Roosevelt, crippled years before by polio, looked tired but greeted his visitors warmly. "Jimmy, I'm proud of you," he said. "All America is proud of you and as their President, it is my privilege to present you with the Medal of Honor for the raid on Tokyo."

Jimmy leaned over as the President placed the star-specked blue ribbon holding a five-pointed star medal around his neck. It was the highest award for bravery in combat that a grateful nation can bestow on a fighting man.

"Thank you, Mr. President," was all Doolittle could think to say.

The citation accompanying the award did not do justice to the deed. It said:

For conspicuous leadership above and beyond the call of duty, involving personal valor and intrepidity at an extreme hazard to life. With the apparent certainty of being forced to land in enemy territory or to perish at sea, General Doolittle personally led a squadron of Army bombers, manned by volunteer crews, in a highly destructive raid on the Japanese mainland.

A few days later, Doolittle was asked to write a narrative of his mission for the benefit of intelligence officers who would study all aspects of the raid and its effects. In his characteristic terse style, dropping the "I," he reported:

"Took off at 8:20 A.M. ship time. Takeoff was easy. Night takeoff would have been possible and practicable.

"Circled carrier to get exact heading and check compass. Wind was from around 300°.

"About a half hour after takeoff, was joined by A/C 40-2292, Lt. Hoover, pilot, the second plane to take off. About an hour out passed a Japanese camouflaged naval surface vessel of about 6,000 tons. Took it to be a light cruiser. About two hours out passed a multimotored land plane headed directly for our flotilla and flying at about 3,000 feet—2 miles away. Passed and endeavored to avoid various civil and naval craft until landfall was made north of Inubo Shuma.

"Was somewhat north of desired course but decided to take advantage of error and approach from a northerly direction, thus avoiding anticipated strong opposition to the west. Many flying fields and the air full of planes north of Tokyo. Most small biplanes apparently primary or basic trainers.

"Encountered nine fighters in three flights of three. This was about ten miles north of the outskirts of Tokyo proper. All this time had been flying as low as the terrain would permit. Continued low flying due south over the outskirts of and toward the east center of Tokyo.

"Pulled up to 1,200 feet, changed course to the southwest, and incendiary-bombed highly inflammable section. Dropped first bomb at 1:30 (ship time).

"Anti-aircraft very active but only one near hit. Lowered away to housetops and slid over western outskirts into low haze and smoke. Turned south and out to sea. Fewer airports on west side but many army posts. Passed over small aircraft factory with a dozen or more newly completed planes on the line. No bombs left. Decided not to machine-gun for reasons of personal security. Had seen five barrage balloons over east central Tokyo and what appeared to be more in the distance.

"Passed on out to sea flying low. Was soon joined by Hoover who followed us to the China coast. Navigator plotted perfect course to pass north of Yaki Shima. Saw three large naval vessels just before passing west end of Japan. One was flatter than the others and may have been a converted carrier. Passed innumerable fishing and small patrol boats.

"Made landfall somewhat north of course on China coast. Tried to reach Chuchow on 4495 (kilocycles) but could not raise.

"It had been clear over Tokyo but became overcast before reaching Yaki Shima. Ceiling lowered on coast until low islands and hills were in it at about 600 feet. Just getting dark and couldn't live under overcast so pulled up to 6,000 feet and then 8,000 feet in it. On instruments from then on, though occasionally saw dim lights on ground through almost solid overcast. These lights seemed more often on our right and pulled us still farther off course.

"Directed rear gunner to go aft and secure films from camera. [Unfortunately, they were jerked out of his shirt front where he had put them when his chute opened.]

"Decided to abandon ship. Sgt. Braemer, Lt. Potter, Sgt. Leonard, and Lt. Cole jumped in order. Left ship on A.F.C.E. (automatic pilot), shut off both gas cocks, and I left. Should have put flaps down. This would have slowed down landing speed, reduced impact, and shortened glide.

"Left airplane about 9:30 P.M. (ship time) after 13 hours in the air. Still had enough gas left for half-hour flight but right front tank was showing empty. Had transferred once as right engine used more fuel. Had covered about 2,250 miles, mostly at low speed, cruising but about an hour at moderate high speed, which more than doubled the consumption for this time.

"All hands collected and ship located by late afternoon of the 19th. Requested General Ho Yang Ling, Director of the Branch Government of Western Chekiang Province, to have a lookout kept along the seacoast from Hang Chow Bay to Wen Chow Bay and also have all sampans and junks along the coast keep a lookout for planes that went down at sea or just reached shore.

"Early morning of 20th, four planes and crews, in addition to ours, had been located and I wired General Arnold, through the Embassy at Chungking: 'Tokyo successfully bombed. Due bad weather on China coast believe all airplanes wrecked. Five crews found safe in China so far.' Wired again on the 27th giving more details.

"Discussed possibility of purchasing three prisoners on the seacoast from Puppet Government and endeavoring to take out the three in the lake area by force. Believe this desire was made clear to General Ku Cho-tung [who spoke little English] and know it was made clear to English-speaking members of his staff. This was at Shangjao. They agreed to try to purchase of three but recommended against force due to large Japanese concentration.

"Bad luck:

(1) Early takeoff due to naval contact with surface and air craft.

(2) Clear over Tokyo.

(3) Foul over China.

"Good luck:

(1) A 25-mph tailwind over most of the last 1,200 miles.

"Takeoff should have been made three hours before daylight, but we didn't know how easy it would be and the Navy didn't want to light up. Dawn takeoff, closer in, would have been better as things turned out. However, due to the bad weather it is questionable if even daylight landing could have been made at Chuchow without radio aid.

"Still feel that original plan of having one plane take off three hours before dusk and others just at dusk was best all-around plan for average conditions."

The summary of Jimmy Doolittle's first combat mission did not completely express his concerns. His first thoughts when he hit the ground were of his own crew and the 75 other men he thought were down somewhere in the vast expanse of China or in the China Sea. He had landed in a rice paddy with knees bent to favor his once-broken ankles that were still sensitive to shock from those days in 1926 in Chile when he had fallen from a window while demonstrating his prowess as an acrobat. He fell into a sitting position neck deep in "night soil" which the Chinese used as fertilizer. Soaking wet and thoroughly cold, he scrambled out and began looking for some signs of habitation. Quentin Reynolds, in his book *The Amazing Mr. Doolittle*, explained what happened next:

"He saw lights in what appeared to be a small farmhouse only a hundred yards away. He unharnessed his 'chute, dropped it, and plodded through the mud of the field to the front door of the house. He banged on it and cried out the Chinese phrase all of the pilots and crewmen had learned, 'Lushu hoo megwa fugi.' (I am an American.) There was an immediate reaction to the phrase, but not the one he had anticipated. He heard a bolt rammed into place on the other side of the door, and at the same time the lights went out. Nothing he could do would arouse the people behind that door.

"Giving up the farmhouse as a bad job, he wandered on. He found a narrow road, followed it half a mile, and then came across a very large box placed on two sawhorses. If he could get inside that box, he would at least be protected from the chill wind. The box was merely covered with planks. He removed them, climbed up on one of the sawhorses, and then hopped down into the box. He found he had company—a very old Chinese gentleman whose hands were folded peacefully on his chest. The Chinese gentleman, however, wasn't asleep; he was dead, and Doolittle assumed, quite correctly, that he had stumbled into a local morgue. Doolittle had no prejudice against spending the night with a dead Chinese, but the box, made out of thin strips of wood, wasn't strong enough to keep out the rising wind. So Doolittle left the dead Chinese and continued up the road.

"He stumbled into an old water mill. The rain had increased now, and the ramshackle mill looked like a real haven. It was relatively dry inside. But he found that the bitter cold kept him from sleeping. He went through a series of bending exercises trying to generate some warmth in his chilled body. He didn't sleep at all that night.

"The morning was overcast, but the rain had stopped. He continued down the road and finally met an old Chinese farmer who looked at him curiously. The farmer spoke no English, nor did he respond to the 'I am an American' phrase, but Doolittle took out a pad and drew a picture of a locomotive on it. When he added a question mark, the farmer smiled and nodded. Evidently there was a railroad somewhere near. The farmer beckoned him to follow. He led him about a mile up the road, not to a railroad but to what was obviously a local Chinese military headquarters. A major who was in charge looked very suspiciously at Doolittle, and held his hand out for Doolittle's .45-caliber gun which he had spotted in its holster. Doolittle shook his head. He found that the major understood English fairly well. He explained that he was an American who had parachuted out of an American plane during the night. He also said that he was an ally of the Chinese army and therefore he would keep his gun.

"There was an uncomfortable silence for a moment while the major and three of his men, cradling tommy guns in their arms, looked at the mud-spattered American. The major hesitated a moment, and Doolittle felt he was on the point of giving an order to have him shot immediately.

" 'I'll lead you to where my parachute is,' he said, and the major nodded.

"Doolittle led them back along the narrow road, past the mill, the morgue, and then he located the farmhouse which had received him so inhospitably the previous night. He found the rice paddy and led them to the exact spot where he had landed. But the parachute he had left there had disappeared.

"The three soldiers were muttering to each other, and the major's eyes showed nothing but disbelief. Doolittle decided that the people in the farmhouse at least would remember the shouting and would remember his banging on the door. He asked the major to check with them. They walked to the farmhouse. The farmer, his wife, and two children looked completely blank when the major interrogated them in rapid Chinese.

" 'They say they heard no noise during the night.' He turned to Doolittle. 'They say they heard no plane during the night. They say they saw no parachute. They say you are lying.'

"Doolittle was now beginning to sweat. He protested vigorously to the major that he was in fact an American officer, that he had bombed Tokyo, and that four members of his crew had bailed out with him. Nothing he said could remove the hard suspicion from the major's eyes. But then two of the soldiers who had gone into the farmhouse reappeared with broad smiles on their faces and the parachute in their arms. Obviously the farmer had thought that the parachute could be converted into something useful. The sight of the parachute completely dissipated the officer's suspicions. He shook hands with Doolittle and immediately ordered his men to get him something to eat. He ordered another to return to headquarters and send out searching parties for Doolittle's crew."

All of Doolittle's crew had survived their bailouts and had similar experiences. Sgt. Paul Leonard had spent the night wrapped in his parachute to keep warm and then walked about six miles the next morning trying to find the other crew members. He later made this report to intelligence officers:

"Returning to where I landed, I encountered four men armed with rifles. One motioned to me to raise my hands while the other three proceeded to cock their rifles. One took aim. At the same moment, I pulled my .45. The one who was aiming fired, so I fired twice. They ran so I turned and climbed to mountaintop where I could see men gathering around the foot of the hill. All of them had rifles. I hid myself as well as possible and they left. I then figured out a course to travel at night.

"After about an hour and a half, I saw a crowd of people returning back down the valley. In front I could see Lt. Potter and Sergeant Braemer. I reloaded my clip because I figured they were captured. I started yelling and ran down the mountain but found they were in good friendly company."

But Potter and Braemer had not been in "good friendly company" when they landed. As soon as they were discovered by a band of guerrillas, they were immediately robbed, tied up, and marched off. Fortunately, they came across an English-speaking Chinese boy who led the guerrillas and their captives to his house and spread the word. Soon the guerrilla chieftain arrived and their belongings were restored. They had set off searching for Leonard when he found them.

Doolittle felt a little better when his crewmen came in, but there were still seventy-five more men to be accounted for. Next day, he made his way back to the scene of the crashed B-25 with Paul Leonard. Potter, who had sprained an ankle in the jump, Cole, and Braemer decided not to go. When the two men arrived at the site, Doolittle's morale reached the lowest point in his entire career. The once-beautiful B-25 was spread all over two acres of mountaintop.

The two men picked through the wreckage and Doolittle found his Army blouse. However, it was oil-soaked, and someone had removed all the brass buttons. That didn't help his morale either. He sat down dejectedly on the airplane with his head in his hands. He described his feelings to the author:

"As I sat there I was very, very depressed. Paul Leonard

took my picture and then, seeing how badly I felt, tried to cheer me up. He said, 'What do you think will happen when you go home, Colonel?'

"I answered, 'Well, I guess they'll send me to Leavenworth.'

"Paul smiled and said, 'No, sir. I'll tell you what will happen. They're going to make you a general.'

"I smiled weakly, and he tried again. 'And they're going to give you the Congressional Medal of Honor,' he said.

"I smiled again, and he made his final effort. 'Colonel,' he said, 'I know they're going to give you another airplane and when they do, I'd like to be your crew chief.'

"It was then that tears came to my eyes, and I told him that if I ever had another airplane and he wanted to be my crew chief, he surely could."

Leonard had no way of knowing that all three of his predictions would come true with uncommon speed, the first two within days. By the time Doolittle reached North Africa to take over his next combat command, he had an airplane designated for his use, a Martin B-26 Marauder, and, true to his promise, Leonard was assigned as its crew chief.

To Doolittle, or any pilot, the request Leonard had made was the highest possible compliment. In February 1943, the two of them landed at a forward Allied airdrome, near Youksles-Bains, Algeria, when it was attacked by German bombers. Doolittle had taken a jeep to a nearby fighter strip, leaving Leonard to work on the plane, when an air-raid alarm sounded. As the German bombers came in low, Leonard manned his plane's top turret guns until the batteries ran down and the turret wouldn't work. He then made a run for an old bomb crater fifty yards away. In one of those soul-tearing freaks of war, a bomb hit the crater just as he reached it and exploded right in his face. In a fraction of a second, the life of the man who had dedicated himself to serving as "the Boss's" crew chief was snuffed out. To Doolittle it was the greatest personal tragedy of the war.

13. North Africa to the Pacific

It Took Military Historians more than twenty years to evaluate the full impact of the Doolittle Raid on the Japanese people. Neither Gen. "Hap" Arnold, who approved the plan for the raid, nor Jimmy Doolittle who flew it, nor President Roosevelt, who afterward presented its leader the Congressional Medal of Honor, would have dared predict that, not only would the raid cause confusion and impede war production briefly but would also have a much greater effect. The entire Japanese offensive war strategy was changed as a direct result of this single air action. And it was this change that encouraged the Japanese to engage American air and naval forces at Midway Island two months later and suffer their first major defeat at the hands of the United States.

Both American and Japanese war historians now concede that the Battle of Midway marked the turning point for Japanese militarism during World War II. It had been sparked by the surprise Doolittle Raid because it encouraged Japanese war leaders to overcommit themselves in battle while underestimating the ability of American air and sea power to fight and win an all-out, pitched battle against numerically superior forces.

It is now acknowledged that the magnificent risks taken by Jimmy Doolittle and his sixteen crews, plus the 10,000 men in the navy task force of sixteen ships, were indeed justified. Because of the psychological impact it had on the Japanese throughout the remainder of the war, Doolittle and his seventy-nine followers proved a point that Gen. Billy Mitchell had made two decades before: airpower possesses the capability to affect the hearts and minds of a real or potential enemy far more than the destructive effect of the bombs carried in bomb bays.

When the news was released that Jimmy Doolittle had been awarded the highest honor that a grateful nation can bestow on a military man, he was hounded by newsmen day and night. Since it had been decided not to release the fact that the bombers had taken off from an aircraft carrier, Jimmy could not answer any questions relating to the takeoff point or their intended destinations in China. Eight men were in the hands of the Japanese and no one knew what suffering they would have to endure if all the facts were made known.

To take advantage of the morale boost that Doolittle had given the nation, General Arnold encouraged him to visit defense factories around the country and give speeches whenever and wherever he could. He made radio talks and appeared on news films to encourage Americans to give their all for the war effort and to make them realize that their military forces could strike back and would be doing it again and again in the months to come.

When the Tokyo Raid moved off the front pages and public interest in Doolittle began to wane, Arnold put him on other special projects and then called him in one day to announce that he was recommending him to Gen. Dwight D. Eisenhower, commander of American forces in England, to organize and command the Twelfth Air Force.

"General Eisenhower has to O.K. you first," Arnold said, "but I don't think there will be any problem. You go ahead to Britain and report to Ike's headquarters."

But there was a problem. When Eisenhower received the nomination from Arnold, he balked. He had never met Doolittle and only knew of him through newspaper stories of his racing victories. While he respected his flying ability and courage, especially since he had won the Medal of Honor, Doolittle had not established any reputation as an organizer in the military. He had been out of the service for ten years and Eisenhower thought anyone who had been away from the military that long would not be familiar with administrative details as then practiced in combat units.

Upon arrival at Eisenhower's headquarters near London, Jimmy made an appointment with the supreme commander. The two men with widely different backgrounds had a long conversation about the future of the war and the concepts for fighting it. Doolittle did not agree with all of his superior's points and told him so. Although the meeting was cordial, it did not go well.

After Doolittle left his office, Eisenhower drafted a message to General Arnold saying he did not want Doolittle to head up the new air force. He asked, instead, for either Generals "Tooey" Spaatz, Tony Frank, or Ira Eaker, three bombing specialists who had served in World War I, had never left the service, and were dedicated army men whom he had known before and who were already in England with the Eighth Air Force.

Arnold cabled Eisenhower: "You can have anyone you want. However, still strongly recommend Doolittle."

It was at this time, the summer of 1942, that an invasion of North Africa was being planned. The Twelfth Air Force, at first called the Twelfth Bomber Command, was to be organized. Many of the Eighth Air Force planes and most experienced crews, making up the principal bomber force in England, were to join the new organization. This disruption of the building up of the Eighth was discouraging and would require someone in charge who knew how to get the most out of men serving under him. At Arnold's urging, Eisenhower reluctantly selected Doolittle to head the Twelfth Air Force and adopted a wait-and-see attitude toward the former racing pilot.

Once assigned the responsibility, Jimmy jumped into the task of organizing with his customary gusto. It was not an easy task to preside over the breaking up of a large air unit that was just beginning to be effective in order to try to build another. It took every bit of tact and persuasion that Doolittle could muster to get what he needed after he had studied the requirements for people, planes, and supplies.

The invasion of North Africa began on November 7, 1942. Doolittle's forces consisted of about 550 fighters and bombers which quickly established themselves, along with their supplies, along the northwest corner of Africa. The basic strategy was to drive eastward, force the Germans and Italians out of North Africa, and eventually defeat the Axis powers in the Mediterranean by pounding away at military targets in Italy.

Although the landing operations went well and few casualties were experienced, Doolittle himself almost didn't get there. Four days before the first Americans were to go ashore, he flew to Gibraltar as a passenger aboard a B-17. The plan was for the plane to fly parallel to the coast of France out of range of German fighters and around Portugal to the British air base at Gibraltar. The *Flying Fortress* was to fly alone, without escort.

The flight was uneventful until the B-17 was off Portugal, where it was attacked by four Luftwaffe JU-88s. The B-17 immediately dove to the wave tops. The attackers followed but had to pull out of their dives carefully or they would splash into the ocean. Bullets laced through the bomber's fuselage as each German attacker made a pass. Luckily, no vital parts were hit, but a stream of bullets smashed into the cockpit and the copilot was wounded. Doolittle, standing in the radio compartment during the attack, rushed forward and helped the navigator ease the copilot out of his seat. After helping to give first aid, Doolittle slipped into the copilot's seat. The pilot, a young lieutenant, thought Doolittle, now wearing the silver star of a brigadier general, wanted to take command of the airplane.

"It's your airplane, son," Doolittle said, anticipating what the young pilot might be thinking. "You're doing a good job."

The German planes broke off the attack and the B-17 flew on to its destination.

During the next three months, the new Air Force made history. Its task was to test the untried and highly controversial principles of air power and to build an air force from scratch in the desert sands of Africa. It was a rehearsal for the inevitable big show that would have to take place in Europe. Once troops were landed, there was no turning back, no failure. Men would die but valuable lessons would be learned that would eventually defeat the Axis powers.

In the crowded weeks that followed, Doolittle's bombers pounded Nazi General Rommel's forces unmercifully and destroyed the German lines of communication and supply. Doolittle, a commander who believed in seeing things for himself, was everywhere. He refused to have an aide assigned and it was probably a good thing because he probably would have worn out dozens of them as they tried to keep up with his fast pace. He flew his own B-26 *Marauder* from base to base, using Sgt. Paul Leonard, his faithful mechanic, as copilot. On bombing missions in the B-17, Doolittle flew as copilot because he believed in seeing the results of the missions with his own eyes. When he made a report to Eisenhower or Arnold, it was not based on the reports of others.

In March 1943 the War Department announced that General Doolittle had been awarded the Air Medal for bombing missions against the enemy. Once more, Doolittle became front page news and newsmen accompanying the Allied troops tried to locate the "Little General," as they had affectionately tagged him. One writer tells what it was like trying to pin Doolittle down for an interview:

In a crowded operations room on a gale-lashed airport which served as Doolittle's headquarters, a reporter dropped in for a chat with Doolittle's executive officer. The latter was wailing because he was in a panic most of the time trying to locate Doolittle. He explained that "the Little General" couldn't be brought to a halt long enough for a conference. And, he said, when you did get the General, he would ponder a second, answer two or three questions with a word, or nod, a gesture or two, and be gone again. The executive said the General didn't seem to know what chairs were made for, because he never sat down. Once within the operations office, Doo-

Sing to your children.

October

3

Sunday

little simply eyed the place in a sweeping glance, and with a soft, friendly grin kept pacing the floor the whole time he spent in the shack.

As he was discussing with the reporter the best method of pinning Doolittle down for a conference, in walked the General. His head was covered by a flier's leather helmet with the ear flaps clipped over his head, and he was wearing a loose leather flying jacket. He strode in quickly. Then he whirled and glanced at names and data posted on the bulletin board, describing the various types of ships out on missions and names of pilots assigned thereto. He took in the information almost at a glance, and ducked out the other door before the executive officer could even catch him on the fly. He left the reporter talking to himself as he trotted out the door after Doolittle.*

In the early months of the war in North Africa, the going was not easy. The Germans put up heavy flak over every target and many American bombers fell to their destruction. The toll on the fliers was heavy and those who survived began to dread the next mission. Morale sank to a dangerously low point.

Doolittle was keenly aware of this as he talked to returning crews. When they spoke of how tough a mission was, Doolittle would nod, give a word of encouragement that the mission had done some good against the enemy, and move on. To the surprise of many crew members, they found that Doolittle had flown on the very missions they had described. At the last minute, he would displace a copilot on a plane scheduled to fly in the rear of a formation. As a result, morale improved and as morale improved so did the teamwork so necessary in air combat.

The amazing Doolittle flew every type of aircraft in his command. He used a British *Spitfire* fighter plane for quick trips between bases but flew twin-engine, B-25s and B-26s from the pilot's seat on actual bombing missions. The young pilots quickly learned that "the Old Man" was no desk general and his personal touch did as much to earn eventual victory as the airplanes they flew and the bombs they dropped.

In the middle of the North African air campaign, an incident

---

* Mann, Carl, *Lightning in the Sky*, p. 254. Robert M. McBride Co., 1943.

The crew of an Eighth Air Force B-17 *Flying Fortess* tells its commanding general what route they will fly on their bombing mission against Germany. Doolittle often flew with combat crews, choosing one shortly before departure. (*Photo courtesy of the U.S. Air Force*)

occurred that Doolittle described as "my greatest personal tragedy of the war":

I landed at a forward airdrome near Youks-les-Bains, Algeria, one
day and I had to go into town to attend to some business with the
ground commanders there. I left Sgt. Paul Leonard to take care of
the plane—a B-26. About midnight that night the Germans came
over and bombed the airfield. I tried to get out there to see if our
plane had been damaged but couldn't because an ammunition dump
had been hit along the road and ammunition was exploding all
over the place.

The next morning I found the airplane. Sergeant Leonard had
moved it to the other side of the field. The plane was there but not
Sergeant Leonard. I found that he had manned the machine gun
turret in the plane as long as the batteries held out and had shot
back at the German planes that were bombing and strafing the airfield. Empty .50-caliber shells were all over the place beneath the
plane.

Finally, I found a bomb crater nearby. It was part of an older
one and I pieced together what had happened. Sergeant Leonard
had fought the attackers as long as he could and then leaped into
the crater for protection. But another bomb, aimed at the plane,
had missed its mark and had hit the old bomb crater instead.

I found what was left of Sergeant Leonard. It was his left hand,
off at the wrist, with a wrist watch still in place. This was all that
remained of the wonderful boy who had tried to cheer me up in
China in my saddest moment.

In the following weeks, as his bombers slowly had their effect
on the supply lines, the German resistance began to crumble.
Doolittle's crews stepped up attacks on the island of Sicily and
on Italy itself. He flew on raids against military targets in Rome
and added the second of the three Axis capitals to his list of
targets. In addition, he scored another aviation "first" that has
seemed to escape public notice.

The tiny island of Pantellino, located between Africa and Sicily, had to be captured before Sicily and Italy could be invaded.
Only 42 square miles in area, it had only one harbor and no

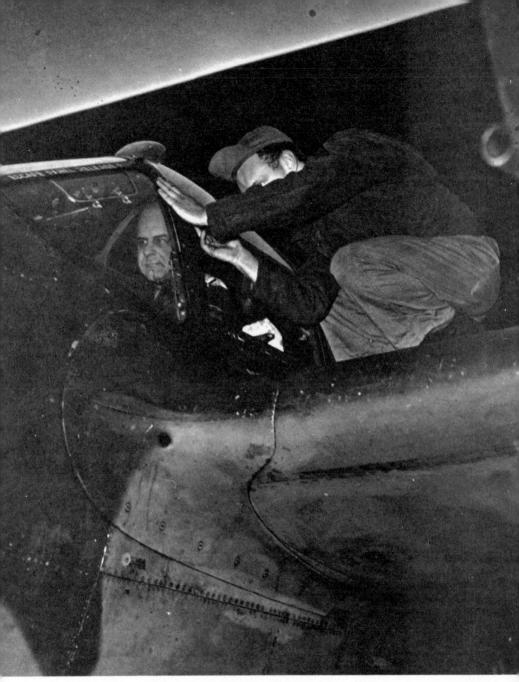

Known as a "flying general," Doolittle flew every type of aircraft assigned to any unit under his command in order to know what fighting crews were experiencing. Here he gets a cockpit checkout in a P-38 *Lightning* before taking off on a test flight. (*Photo courtesy of the U.S. Air Force*)

beaches on which barges could be landed easily. German 88's—
heavy flak guns that scored heavily against American planes—
were located all over the island and photo planes had located
over one hundred gun emplacements in strategic positions.

Doolittle reasoned that this difficult piece of enemy territory
provided an opportunity to test the theory that air power, properly applied, could break the will of an enemy to resist. There
were 15,000 Italian troops there who were going to exact a tremendous toll of Allied ground forces scheduled to assault the
island fortress.

Doolittle ordered his fighters and bombers to attack Pantellino
with everything they had. Heavy bombers came at high altitudes
with heavy loads and dropped them on large targets such as
supply dumps. Medium bombers came in lower and aimed at the
smaller targets. The fighters came in on the deck and strafed
anything that moved. The attacks went on around the clock for
several days. The invasion force was scheduled to land on June
12, 1943. But, from intelligence reports, it didn't appear as if the
best efforts of Doolittle's pilots had been good enough. Commanders of American ground troops reluctantly prepared for heavy
losses when their forces stormed ashore.

While the landing forces set out from North Africa and
steamed for the island, Doolittle's forces prepared to fly top
cover. The day before the invasion, however, his pilots returned
to report that a huge white cross had been painted on the runway of the island's only airport. A white flag flying from a hill
overlooking the harbor was seen by the invasion force. The Italians had surrendered to Allied airpower before a single American went ashore!

But not all of Doolittle's missions were so successful. In fact,
he refers to one as the "most disappointing" experience he had
during World War II. It concerned a report that the Italian
battleship *Roma*, two large cruisers, and a few smaller vessels
were located in the harbor at La Spezia. It was important that
they be prevented from leaving to attack Allied naval units. Doolittle describes what happened:

We planned an operation against these ships in which we sent three groups of 36 planes each. One group was to attack the *Roma*, the other two were to go after the two cruisers. The planes carried 1600-pound armor-piercing bombs and 2000-pound demolition bombs.

I led the operation and the flight in and out was fairly uneventful. When we developed reconnaissance pictures after the mission, we found that one cruiser hadn't been hit at all and the other had only a forward turret knocked off by a 2000-pound bomb. The *Roma* itself had an armor-piercing bomb go through the hull and come out the bottom without exploding.

Although three groups had been put on the raid to be sure the job was done, we had accomplished virtually nothing. That was the most disappointing raid I ever participated in and was made more disappointing because later, when the Italians tried to turn the *Roma* over to the British at Malta, one single German plane with a radar-controlled bomb sank it.

Whatever Doolittle may have thought of his failures, the successes he had, the personal brand of leadership he exhibited, and the never-ending drive to accomplish his job did not go unnoticed in high places. He had shown that he could lead men, that he could get along with his ground and naval counterparts, and that he could do his part to help the Allies win the Mediterranean back from the Axis.

His reward came in the form of a transfer at the end of 1943 to command the Eighth Air Force. Another reward came in the form of a short note. It said:

Dear Jimmy:

When you joined me in London you had much of what it takes to exercise high command. I am not exaggerating when I tell you that in my opinion you have shown during the past year the greatest degree of improvement of any of the senior United States officers serving in my command. You are every day rendering services of inestimable value to our country.

Sincerely,
Eisenhower

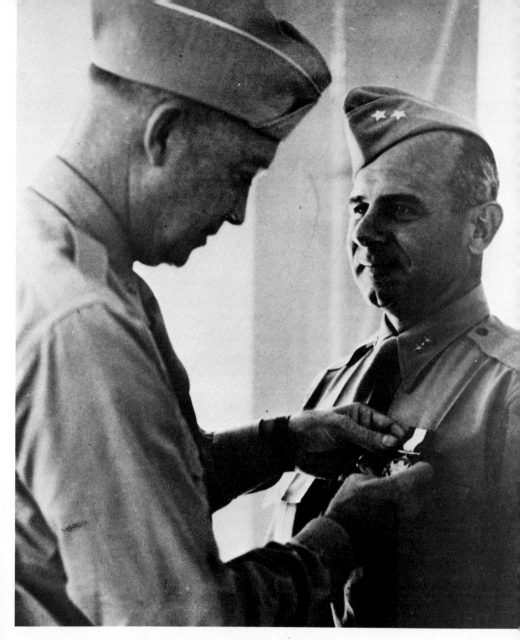

Doolittle received the Distinguished Service Medal from Gen. Dwight D. Eisenhower for his service as commander of Air Force units operating in North America. He was subsequently promoted to lieutenant general and transferred to command the Eighth Air Force in England.

Doolittle arrived in England in January 1944, just as the "mighty Eighth" was mounting its attacks on the Luftwaffe. The targets chosen for attack by the Eighth's bombers were the German fighters and fighter-bombers in the air and on the ground, their assembly plants, and the factories that made the components that went into these planes.

By this time, the German high command had withdrawn the bulk of its fighter defenses to the great industrial districts inside Germany, leaving only a modest number of fighters in the probable invasion areas. With the invasion set for June 1944, the Eighth Air Force, in combination with other Allied air strength, was committed to a bombing program to insure its success. The list of targets was expanded to include strategic rail centers, coastal defense batteries, naval installations, and oil refineries.

The campaign was so successful that General Eisenhower was able to tell the troops about to embark for the invasion of France: "If you see any planes, don't worry; they'll be ours."

Through the air campaign before and after the invasion, Doolittle continued his "see-and-be-seen" techniques. He flew on missions whenever he could and there was little that he didn't know about the command he had inherited.

During the year after he arrived, Doolittle was promoted to lieutenant general and thus scored another first—the first reserve officer ever to attain three-star rank. There was no change in the man as his military rank increased, however. He had acquired an aide but still didn't want one. He still was to be found everywhere personally searching out problems and solving them.

One story is told about this period that shows that the aggressive spirit of the former boxing champion carried over to the task before him as commander of the Eighth. On one of his visits to a fighter command, he saw signs in the operations shacks that read: "The first duty of Eighth Air Force fighters is to bring the bombers back alive."

"Who said so?" Doolittle asked one of his generals.

The general shrugged and replied, "That's the word from up above," meaning that Doolittle's predecessor had given this as a

Eighth Air Force generals plan the air war against Germany. Left to right: Brig. Gen. Charles Y. Banfill, director of intelligence; Maj. Gen. Orvil A. Anderson, deputy commanding general for operations; and Doolittle, commander. (*Photo courtesy of the National Archives*)

guiding philosophy for the Eighth's fighter pilots whenever they had a choice to make.

"Get those signs down right away and put up new ones," Doolittle ordered. "Make them read 'The first duty of our fighters is to destroy German fighters!'"

From that moment on, American fighter pilots took the offensive as they had not done before. While some fighters always covered the bombers, the bulk of the fighter force went after the German interceptors with a vengeance in the air and on the ground.

As the fighters stepped up their attacks and assumed the offensive, the bombers shifted their targets to the German oil industry since fuel was the enemy's prime necessity. The increased bombing tempo, as Allied units pushed across France after the invasion, played havoc with the enemy's efforts to move men and war materials to the front lines. Estimated oil production of the Germans dropped from 1,350,000 metric tons in April 1944 to about 300,000 metric tons as Allied ground forces approached the German border. By March 1945 it was obvious that the complete collapse of the German army, now almost without fuel and no longer mobile, was not far off.

During this period, Doolittle flew on missions but "Ike" Eisenhower wouldn't let him fly into Germany so that, in spite of stories to the contrary, he did not bomb Berlin and does not claim to be the only pilot to have attacked all three Axis capitals.

One story is told about the assault on Germany that gives further insight into the man named Doolittle. Toward the end of the war in Europe, bombing by the use of radar was being perfected. This permitted bombardiers to attack targets covered by clouds. However, it was not as accurate then as now and best results were always achieved when targets could be bombed "visually."

On one important mission, a formation leader was ordered to proceed to an alternate target if, when approaching the primary target, he thought it would be covered by clouds. But the primary target was the more important of the two and its destruction would help to shorten the war drastically.

Not many generals had the honor of pinning medals on their sons. Here, Lieutenant General Doolittle, pinch-hitting for a Ninth Air Force commander, pins the Distinguished Flying Cross on his eldest son, Jimmy, Jr., now deceased. Jimmy, Jr., earned the award for medium bomber sorties against the enemy in Europe. (*Photo courtesy of U.S. Air Force*)

As the formation proceeded to the primary target over a solid undercast, there appeared to be no end to the clouds. The leader, impatient to get the job over with, felt it was useless to proceed to the primary target and turned his formation toward the secondary. As he did so, he radioed the course change to his base in England.

Almost immediately, a voice came over the radio. "This is Queen Bee," it said. "You will bomb your primary target. Repeat, you will bomb your primary target."

"Queen Bee" was the call sign for Doolittle that day and the formation leader assumed that Doolittle was back at his headquarters listening on the radio. He replied: "Proceeding to secondary as directed due to clouds over primary."

The reply to this was sharp and unmistakably Doolittle's voice.

"There is one of our fighters orbiting primary target area your altitude. Target is clear and can be bombed visually. You will proceed to primary."

The formation leader turned back on course and found, to his surprise, that the clouds parted as he neared the primary target. Just as his bombardier called "bomb doors open!" he spotted a lone P-47 *Thunderbolt* circling the area. As the bombs dropped, the fighter wagged its wings and streaked for home. Official records do not show who was piloting the fighter that day but ask anyone who served in the Eighth Air Force during those days and they'll tell you.

The attacks against the enemy by the Eighth Air Force have been examined closely by historians. In the 995 days between its first mission on August 17, 1942, and the German surrender on May 8, 1945, its planes had mounted ever-increasing attacks against Nazi airplane factories and airfields, oil refineries, submarine pens, railroads and water transportation networks, flying bomb and rocket-launching sites, military installations, and many other strategic and tactical targets. Tens of thousands of American, British, and Russian lives were saved because bombing attacks by the Eighth prevented Nazi submarines from being launched, planes from taking off, locomotives and trucks from having the fuel to haul supplies and ammunition for use against Allied troops.

In the weary months he had been away, the ever-busy Doolittle had not been too busy to write to his faithful wife, Jo. One day toward the end of 1944 he wrote her a letter which she later released because it expressed some significant thoughts of her husband's that she thought should be shared. He wrote:

Cold weather, shorter days, and soon another year gone. How time flies—and this in spite of the constant desire to get the job done and return home to loved ones. Sometimes tired, particularly when things go wrong. Rested, refreshed and exhilarated when things are going smoothly. Responsibility! Responsibility to God, nation, superiors, contemporaries, subordinates and self.

Command, regardless of its size of importance, carries with it both responsibility and opportunity. Responsibility to superiors and subordinates. Opportunity to utilize to advantage one's attributes and ability. It is difficult but necessary to exercise command in such a way as to assure the respect and loyalty of subordinates and the confidence of superiors. To strive to avoid engendering antagonism and annoyance and establish approbation, admiration and even affection. The last objective is rarely achieved; particularly among our contemporaries.

I sometimes think that when this is all over I'd like to run a peanut stand. Would want it on a quiet street where there wouldn't be too many customers to interfere with my meditations. Actually, after about a week's rest, I imagine I'd be restless and looking for work and responsibility.

As the war in Europe came to its conclusion, Doolittle did get a week's rest. He received orders to move his Eighth Air Force headquarters to the Pacific and was to proceed via Washington, where Jo had been patiently waiting out the weeks and months for him to return. The week's rest was all he needed. Faced with a new task of reorganizing the Eighth, he knew that much work lay ahead. The primary airplane would now be the new B-29 *Superfortress*, which had not been used over Europe. Larger and faster than the B-17 *Flying Fortress* and the B-24 *Liberator*, it

Jimmy Doolittle was transferred from Europe to the South Pacific in the Spring of 1945. Here he greets crewmen of the first B-29 *Super Fortress* to arrive in Okinawa. (*Photo courtesy of the National Archives*)

Shortly after being given command of B-29's in the South Pacific, the "flying-est general in the Air Force," checked out in the left seat. (*Photo courtesy of the National Archives*)

could carry heavier bomb loads. Doolittle was to establish his headquarters on Okinawa and be ready as soon as possible to mount attacks against the Japanese home islands.

The amassing of Allied air power against the home islands of Japan spelled the end of the war in the Far East. Their forces slowly disintegrated as increasing B-29 strength enabled the Americans to bomb round-the-clock. Many Japanese leaders knew it was only a matter of time before they must surrender.

But a hard core of Japanese militarists refused to give in. For them it took two fatal blows before they, too, realized that the end of their fanatical dreams had come. The first occurred on August 6, 1945, when a single B-29, the *Enola Gay*, dropped a single bomb on Hiroshima. The second came three days later when another B-29, *Bock's Car*, repeated the performance at Nagasaki.

The next day, the Japanese government decided that further resistance was useless. Jimmy Doolittle, along with many other army, navy, and air force leaders who had fought so long, was invited to the surrender ceremony aboard the battleship *Missouri* on Sunday, September 2, 1945—three years, eight months, and twenty-five days after the attack on Pearl Harbor. There, Japanese leaders penned their signatures to the articles of surrender and World War II was officially over.

As Doolittle stood on the *Missouri's* deck, he thought about the harsh months that he had survived and was deeply glad it was all over. He had risen from the grade of major to lieutenant general. He had commanded the mightiest bombing force the world had ever known. He had received the nation's highest honor for heroism "above and beyond the call of duty." But the accomplishment that he was personally proudest of was not the number of bombs his planes had dropped or the extent of damage inflicted on the Axis. It was a technical judgment he had made shortly after he had resigned his regular commission and started the aviation division for Shell Oil Company. That judgment was that Shell should lead the way in producing 100-octane gasoline.

An important date in the history of the Shell Oil Company was

April 30, 1934, when a plant in Illinois produced the first 1,000 gallons of 100-octane gasoline under an army contract. During World War II, on the tenth anniversary of that event, *The New York Times* had printed an editorial entitled "Anniversary of Power." It is a tribute to the foresight and courage of an uncommon man:

Ten years ago today, 1,000 gallons of 100-octane gasoline, the first ever to be produced in commercial quantities, was delivered by the Shell Oil Company to the Army Air Corps at Wright Field. The company commemorates that anniversary by opening its new twin catalytic cracking plant for the manufacture of high-octane gasoline at Wood River, Ill., and the Petroleum Administrator for War, the Army and the Navy will inaugurate tomorrow the national celebration of 100-Octane Week. There can be little question that fuel of 100-octane or better rating, set down in high quantities for our Air Force and Navy fliers around the world, has been one of the vital underlying factors in our superiority over the enemy. The margin in speed and performance provided by such gasoline has heavily weighted the odds in our favor and saved hundreds of lives.

Many details of the wartime advances in petroleum technology, especially in relation to high-octane, must still remain on the confidential list, but it is a matter of record and a tribute to the petroleum industry that constant improvement in quality and reduction in price have accompanied the development. The first 1,000-gallon shipment delivered from California to Ohio ten years ago cost $2.40 a gallon. Today the price to the air services in bulk is less than the motorist pays for his day-by-day fuel at the roadside pump. Many companies and individuals have shared in the achievement represented by our dominance in high-octane fuel. It should not be forgotten, however, that among the many debts which American airpower owes to Lieutenant General Doolittle is his insistence a decade ago, when, as a civilian, he was in charge of the aviation development of Shell, that his company carry on energetically research in 100-octane gasoline.

14. "A Pattern of Purpose and Consistence"

THE END OF THE greatest war ever fought was a time for men to pick up the pieces of their lives. Thousands of men were released from the services within a short time and contemplated their personal futures. Jimmy Doolittle was no exception. Although he was the highest-ranking reserve officer on active duty and plans were in the works to establish a separate air force equal in status to the army and navy, he felt that he should see if Shell Oil Company still wanted him. After all, he had told them when he went back in uniform in 1940 that it was only for the duration of the war he knew was coming. Now that it was over, he felt obligated to return.

The Shell people not only wanted him back but they wanted him back in a higher position than he had when he left. He was offered the job of vice president. His duties, if he accepted, would be as a troubleshooter and problem-solver. The idea appealed to Doolittle but he had to add a condition to his acceptance.

"The air force is going to be a separate service one of these days," he told Shell officials, "and there are difficult days ahead as it tries to break away from the army and set up its own organization. I'm going to keep my reserve status and may be called back for various short-term assignments to help out. Will Shell go along with this possibility?"

Shell could and did. Jimmy shed his uniform in the fall of 1945 and moved to a plush office in New York City. As soon as he slipped behind his desk, he began dropping notes to the men who had flown with him on the Tokyo Raid. He reminded the sixty-one men who had survived the war that he had made a promise to them before they had left the *Hornet* in April 1942. The promise was that "when we get to Chungking, I'm going to throw you fellows the biggest party you ever saw."

Recalled back to the states soon after the raid, he couldn't keep that promise at the time. But the war was over now and that promise had to be kept. "Meet me in Miami and help me celebrate my birthday," he said.

Everyone who got the message accepted, including the four men who had survived forty months of solitary confinement at the hands of the Japanese. Doolittle arranged with a Miami hotel to have a large block of rooms set aside in December 1945, and one by one, from all over the country, the Tokyo Raiders showed up "to help the Boss celebrate his birthday."

It cost Doolittle more than $2,000 out of his own pocket to make good on the promise he had made aboard the *Hornet*. The raiders had such a good time that one of them suggested, "Let's do this every year!" Jimmy replied, "I'd like that, fellas, but I'm afraid I couldn't afford it. From here on, it's up to you to carry the ball."

No reunion was held in 1946, but Miami again echoed to the jokes and reminiscenses of Doolittle's Tokyo Raiders in 1947. With the war two years behind them now, they relaxed completely, much to the dismay of the hotel's night watchman. His report to the manager said:

> The Doolittle boys added some gray hairs to my head. This has been the worst night since I worked here. They were completely out of my control.
>
> I let them make a lot of noise but when about fifteen of them went into the pool at 1:00 A.M., including Doolittle, I told them

there was no swimming allowed at night. They were in the pool until 2:30 A.M.

I went up twice more without results. They were running around in the halls in their bathing suits and were noisy until 5:00 A.M. Yes, it was a rough night.

The hotel manager was not at all disturbed by the night watchman's report. He asked Doolittle and his raiders to auto-graph the report so that he would have a souvenir of their visit. As far as he was concerned, they had earned the right to make all the noise they wanted to make in his hotel. He was proud to have had them as his guests.

The Tokyo Raiders have met almost each year since they first gathered in Miami so that "the Boss" could keep his promise. The reunions are still lighthearted affairs but instead of the Raiders paying for their stay, the group has met in various cities from coast to coast as guests of prominent members of the com-munity, civic organizations, and private industry.

The tone of the three-day gatherings has changed over the years. Although they met originally only for fun and fellowship, they now have three purposes in mind: to renew their friendship, to honor the memory of those who have passed on, and to partic-ipate in some activity which is of benefit to the community in which they meet, the Air Force, and the nation.

The agreement Doolittle had with Shell whereby he would be free to help out if the nation called on him was soon tested. In 1946 he was asked to serve on the Secretary of War's Board on Officers/Enlisted Men Relationships. Known as the Doolittle Board, it had developed because of complaints by World War II enlisted men of ill treatment at the hands of officers. The recom-mendations that the Board made were highly controversial be-cause old-line military officers thought they would result in a poorly disciplined military establishment. When asked about his assessment of the board twenty years later, Doolittle replied:

The report was fairly well accepted at the time but was bitterly criticized later. You must remember that this occurred shortly

The famous Gen. "Jimmy" Doolittle is happiest when he is with his Tokyo Raiders at their annual reunions. He is shown here with two of the crew members who had been prisoners of the Japanese, the late George Barr (right), and Chase J. Nielson (center).

Jimmy Doolittle married Josephine Daniels in December 1917. They are shown at a recent reunion of Doolittle's Tokyo Raiders where both are always honored guests.

after the end of World War II which we thought was a war to end wars. The public was fed up with the military, fed up with war, fed up with discipline.

Take saluting, for example. It was found that very frequently enlisted men didn't choose to salute officers away from a military post, and it was very difficult to make them do so. One of our recommendations was that saluting would be obligatory on post and optional off post. This brought a great deal of criticism. The recommendation was made, not because the committee members didn't believe that saluting was desirable on and off post, but that it was felt you couldn't enforce the rule in the light of public reaction to the military and to war at that time.

Controversial or not, the military services adopted most of the recommendations of the Doolittle Board and Doolittle returned to his Shell office. However, he was soon recalled to active duty to serve on a Joint Congressional Aviation Policy Board, followed by appointment to a Committee on National Security Organization. These appointments were followed in later years by service on the Air Force Scientific Advisory Board, the President's Foreign Intelligence Advisory Board, and the National Advisory Committee for Aeronautics, the President's Science Advisory Committee, and similar groups that wanted his expertise.

During his postwar years with Shell, he continued flying Air Force aircraft and the company-owned B-25 to make his many cross-country trips. He checked out in jets, including the F-100, first U.S. supersonic fighter, the KC-135 jet tanker, and B-47 and B-52 jet bombers.

After forty years in the cockpit, however, Doolittle finally decided to quit flying altogether. "I decided this because I saw what happened to my friends who only half-quit," he said. "They flew less and less and didn't stay proficient. Inevitably, they would be tempted to go into bad weather and they ended up dead. When I found that I could not fly enough to stay proficient, I decided to quit and I did."

Jimmy Doolittle may have decided to quit flying as pilot but not as passenger. He has traveled millions of miles on the world's airlines as he jumps from place to place to keep appointments. He is on the board of a number of companies and is constantly in demand as a consultant and participant in the aviation affairs of the Free World.

A typical contribution to public service made by Doolittle came in 1952 when President Harry S Truman appointed him head of a three-man commission "to look into the problem of airport location and use." In a "Dear Jim" letter, the President expressed his distress "about airplane accidents, both commercial and military, that have occurred in the takeoff and landing of aircraft, especially in heavily populated areas." He added: "I have been concerned about the loss of life and I have been concerned about the anxiety in some of our cities" and asked Doolittle to come up with a study "that is both objective and realistic."

In typical "can do" fashion, Doolittle went to work. With the other two members, Charles F. Horne, Civil Aeronautics Administrator, and Dr. Jerome C. Hunsaker, head of the Massachusetts Institute of Technology's Aeronautical Engineering Department, he made his report to the President within the required 90 days. The commission had consulted with 264 individuals and received written or oral statements from 42 others.

In the report, a characteristic "Doolittleism" appears concerning the dangers inherent in aviation: "The 'calculated risk' is an American concept which gives mobility to the whole social structure," the report notes. "The phrase simply means a willingness to embark deliberately on a course of action which offers prospective rewards outweighing its estimated dangers. The American public accepts the calculated risk of transportation accidents as an inescapable condition to the enjoyment of life in a mechanical age. However, the public expects and cooperates to obtain a continuing diminution of avoidable accidents so as to narrow the gap between relative and absolute safety."

The Doolittle Commission made 25 recommendations, many of them so forward-looking that it has taken many years to put them into effect. A few of them have not been heeded to this day, such as adequate zoning around airports, integrated municipal and airport planning, airport improvements to keep up with the state of the construction and electronic arts,' and positive air-traffic control. Midair collisions, which have occurred over the years with nightmarish frequency, could be avoided if the Commission's recommendations, such as minimizing training and test flights at congested airports, separation of military and civil flying at crowded airports, and the avoidance of military training over congested areas, had been put into effect.

Doolittle's interest in military and international affairs has not diminished with the years. Always an advocate of strong military forces, he was one of the founders of the Air Force Association, a nonprofit organization dedicated to maintaining an air force second to none other in the world. At the annual meeting of the association in 1978, the 75th anniversary of powered flight, he was asked to make the keynote address. He took the opportunity to review the progress of U.S. military aviation and express his genuine concern about its future:

"Historians keep reminding us that, over many centuries, mankind suffered from what could be called 'Bird Envy.' That is, while man was inspired by the ability of birds to fly, he also was frustrated by his own inability to emulate them.

"Back in 1908 a 41-year-old pilot put it this way: 'I sometimes think,' he said, 'that the desire to fly after the fashion of birds is an ideal handed down to us by our ancestors who look enviously on the birds soaring freely through space . . . on the infinite highway of the sky.'

"The speaker was Wilbur Wright.

"And yet, when he and brother Orville, just five years earlier, had demonstrated the means by which man—at long last—could *out*fly the birds on the so-called 'highway of the sky,' their achievement was virtually ignored.

"The key to beating the birds, of course, was not only *power* for flight, but a way to *control* a flying machine in speed, direction, and altitude. It was the combination of these factors, long sought by many people, that the Wright Brothers demonstrated successfully 75 years ago at Kitty Hawk.

"The historic significance of that first flight was only dimly perceived by the Wrights themselves. It was not sensed at all by our government, nor the press, nor the public, *nor* the military.

"Yet, it should be noted that after five years of persistent promoting by the Wrights to sell our government on their invention—the sale was justified as a military requirement. And so the early years in the practical use of powered flight were largely devoted to military development and operations.

"The Aviation Section of the Army's Signal Corps was established in 1907 to explore and exploit the potential of the airship and the flying machine for military purposes.

"As the first step, a nonrigid airship and the Wright Brothers' powered 'Flyer' were delivered in August of 1908 . . . and historians report that the airship was considered to have much more potential.

"In this regard, isn't it ironical that in this 75th anniversary year of powered flight, the outstanding flight of the year will quite likely be the nonpowered first crossing of the Atlantic by a free balloon. If that shakes you, consider that it took several centuries for the balloon to accomplish what the airplane did in less than 25 years.

"Another candidate is the man-powered plane now in the Smithsonian.

"At any rate, when we entered World War One in 1917, the United States stood 14th in air strength among the nations of the world. Not much to boast about for the inventors of powered flight.

"The United States came out of World War One with a batch of obsolete aircraft, but with a cadre of well-trained

General James H. "Jimmy" Doolittle and Colonel Carroll V. Glines auto-
graph copies of *Doolittle's Tokyo Raiders* and *Four Came Home* during a
reunion of the famous flyer with the B-25 crews he led on the historic raid
against Japan in April 1942. Autographs of the surviving Tokyo Raiders are
highly prized by collectors and World War II history buffs.

Commercial aviation owes much to these four men who were present at the 50th anniversary of Jimmy Doolittle's historic aviation "first"—the first blind flight in history, which took place at Mitchell Field, New York on September 24, 1929. Pictured (left to right) are Paul Kollsman, inventor of the Kollsman sensitive barometric altimeter used on the flight; Lt. Gen. Jimmy Doolittle; Dr. Lewis M. Hull, former president of Aircraft Radio and Control Co. and director of studies that resulted in the beacon equipment used; and Brig. Gen. Benjamin S. Kelsey, safety pilot on the experimental flights and later head of the Air Force All-Weather Flying Division. A reenactment of the flight was made on September 24, 1979 at Boonton, New Jersey. (Photo by C. V. Glines)

pilots and mechanics and, most important, with a new enthusiasm about the limitless potential of aviation.

"In the earlier postwar period, an aeronautical exposition was held in Madison Square Garden to display the many varieties of planes that had come out of the war. An editorial writer summed up his impressions of the event in these words:

" 'We are literally and without exaggeration on the threshold of a new age whose developments the most imaginative can hardly forecast . . . The dominion of the air has been won, and securely won; and the whole direction of our life is likely to be changed in consequence.'

"This viewpoint may have been shared by a number of people, but the leaders of our military establishment were not among them.

"In 1920 the Air Service was established as a branch of the Army. But except for this small step and the Army's remarkable round-the-world flight in 1924, the decade could from a military viewpoint be called the 'terrible twenties.'

"The most sensational event was the court-martial of Billy Mitchell.

"Yet, the major impact of the court-martial was not that it censured Mitchell, but that it dramatized the need to modernize our military thinking. And it stimulated our young creative airmen to begin forging a new airpower concept for the nation.

"The court-martial did more. It proved the need for organized *public* support of airpower—a lesson not lost on Major Henry H. (Hap) Arnold, who was exiled to a cavalry post for his support of Mitchell. Some 20 years later, in the wake of World War Two, Arnold—then a five-star General—called for the establishment of this organization, the Air Force Association, to fill the gap in public support Mitchell had experienced. Thus, the heritage of the Air Force Association dates back to Billy Mitchell.

"Out of the studies stimulated by Mitchell's experience came the concept of the air ocean, projections of technical progress that would give airpower global reach, the necessity for air superiority, and blueprints for strategic air power, among other ideas.

"When the time came to implement a strategy against the aggression of the Axis powers, the Air War Plan—shaped up in the late twenties and early thirties—became *the* War Plan for the Allies.

"But the equipment was not available to implement the plan. As Hap Arnold commented on Germany's invasion of Poland in 1939: 'During all the years since World War One we have had time and no money. Now we will have money and no time.'

"Beginning with orders from Britain and France, our aviation industry and later our automobile industry gave us the start toward mass production of aircraft and armament. In the end we prevailed by simply outnumbering the enemy in the air and by superior employment of airpower.

"But let's never forget that Germany meanwhile had introduced the world to the rocket plane, to jet aircraft and to prototypes of the guided missile. Nor should it be forgotten that we achieved jet flight as a result of a gift of the Whittle engine from Great Britain. In short, we were badly outgunned on the technological front.

"To make matters worse, within the decade following World War Two, the Soviet Union introduced the world to space flight, to man in orbit, to the Intercontinental Ballistic Missile.

"We must not downgrade our own technological achievements over the years—among them, powered flight itself . . . air-ground communications . . . instrument flying . . . in-flight refueling . . . inertial guidance . . . supersonic flight . . . a revolution in strategic airlift. At the same time we cannot afford one iota of complacency. We cannot again survive the kind of technological inferiority we experienced in World War Two, and that means we must promptly get on the R&D ball. We are rapidly falling behind.

"Not only are we in a highly competitive business, but

we can be our own worst enemy. I believe, for example, that we blundered in canceling the supersonic transport even though the economic conditions for our airlines were not favorable—that we blundered badly in canceling the B-1. We cannot abide complacency.

"Our commercial aircraft are superb—the envy of the world. For years our commercial airliners were adaptations of military transports. Now we're buying industry-designed and -financed aircraft—particularly the widebodied jets—for military use. A healthy sign.

"We are beginning to see the day—long dreamed of—when low-cost mass commercial air transportation will place all corners of the earth within the reach of everyone who can afford to buy a bus ticket to and from work.

"Powered flight has had an impact far beyond transportation itself. An editorial in *Air Force* magazine is quite right in stating that 'Powered Flight has been a principal catalyst in the scientific-technical revolution that has changed the world.'

"Where do we go next in the revolution? Well, I'm not one to hedge, but experience tells me anything I might say, no matter how far-fetched it might seem, quite probably would be an understatement. Consider the following:

"In 1878 Frederick Engels—the founding father of communism—stated that the weapons used in the Franco-Prussian War had reached such a state of perfection that further progress of a revolutionary nature was no longer possible. Thirty some years later the following unforeseen systems were used in World War One: aircraft, tanks, chemical weapons, trucks, submarines, and radio communications.

"A 1937 study entitled 'Technological Trends and National Policy' failed to foresee the following systems, each operational by 1957: jet engines, radar, inertial navigation, nuclear weapons, nuclear-powered submarines, rocket power, missiles, electronic computers, and the general use of pilotless aircraft and helicopters.

"The 1945 Von Karman study entitled 'New Horizons' was a superb effort but it missed the following, each operational within 15 years: solid-state electronics, ICBMs, man in space.

"All this underscores the dynamic, complex, and challenging nature of our mission.

"It means that we have a job to do, now and in the foreseeable future, that is bigger, more complicated, more important than ever before.

"When the Air Force Association was established back in 1946, we centered our efforts on one goal—establishment of a separate and independent Air Force—official recognition that a third dimension had been added to national survival. Airpower was simpler in those days—and so were the issues.

"What stands clear in my mind is the overriding need in this complicated world for accurate, timely information on the issues that can make or break this nation. Not just issues of parochial Air Force interest, but those which affect the whole fabric of international relations.

"I close with these words of the late Gill Robb Wilson [a noted aviation writer]—words which give special meaning to all the movement of men and machines during the first 75 years of powered flight.

" 'Centuries hence,' said Gill, 'the historian will frame the American airman as the pioneer, not alone of flight, but of an intellectual and spiritual process which overcame static and divisive forces, and opened the way to realization of a common humanity—meanwhile preserving the people from conquest.'

"To that noble end we are dedicated."

The fabulous Jimmy Doolittle is now in the eighth decade of his busy life. He has become an elder statesman whose wise counsel and guidance are sought in every phase of aviation and aerospace science.

As he looks back over his busy years as a military and racing pilot, he has formed a personal philosophy about life that is both

Jimmy Doolittle (second from left) knew all of the "greats" of aviation. Here he chats with Charles A. Lindbergh (right) and two airline pilots on the occasion of Lindbergh's induction as an Honorary Member of the Air Line Pilots Association in 1969. Doolittle was inducted in 1971.

refreshing and unique. As an air-age pioneer, his experience gives him the credentials to reflect on modern-day life and predict the future.

"My philosophy of life is really quite simple," he told the author. "I believe every person has been put on this earth for just one purpose: to serve his fellow man. It doesn't matter how he does this. He can build a bridge, paint a picture, invent a labor-saving gadget, or run a gas station. The point is, he should try to leave the earth a better place than he found it. If he does, his life will have been worthwhile. If he doesn't do what he can within his own limitations, he is destined to be unhappy."

Jimmy Doolittle's whole adult life has been spent following this philosophy. From the day he first tried to fly, he has pursued each task and duty with the objective of doing something constructive to solve a problem or improve a situation. His career has been called "a pattern of purpose and consistence" in which he has never stopped trying to make the world he touches a better place for future generations.

There has, perhaps, been a bit of luck attached to his career as a flier. He crashed a number of times but always escaped unscathed. He doesn't think of himself as a bold, super-brave pilot either. "I have always tried to be conservative," he said. "I've always tried to do something new, but before exhibiting that new thing before the public, I practiced it again and again to be sure the hazard was minimized as much as possible. My calculations didn't always work out precisely, however. Otherwise, I wouldn't have had to jump out of an airplane three times to save my neck," he said, smiling.

Because of his status as an elder statesman of aviation, Jimmy Doolittle, while he doesn't like to talk, is often called upon to make speeches to civic, educational, and government groups. He gave one at a Florida junior college that expresses his observations about America as he sees it today. He said:

Obviously, we are the greatest and the finest nation in the world and the leader of the free world.

Great changes have taken place in the last two hundred years and the rate of change is increasing.

Some of the changes in our environment are obvious.

We have gone from a few people to many. Our population is still more than doubling every fifty years. In the year 1800, it was just over five million. In 1900, it was almost 76 million. In the year 2000 it is anticipated that there will be over 300 million people in the United States.

We have gone from a largely agricultural society to a largely industrialized society. This has caused a movement of workers to the industrial centers and has resulted in crowded metropolises. Those metropolitan centers were not originally properly planned for continuing growth, thus adding to the ensuing congestion.

In a word, our environment has changed from one of freedom to one of restriction.

The word "freedom" epitomized our great Nation. We must continue to espouse freedom—and everything it represents—but we must not forget the obligations that go with freedom. With individual freedom goes the obligation to protect the rights of others. We must protect the rights of the individual but, at the same time, must also protect the rights and the security of the body politic.

With it all has come prosperity and, for a majority of our people, the highest standard of living the world has ever known.

Unfortunately, some of our people have not participated, to the full, in this prosperity.

This environmental change, naturally, has caused some change in our people.

Changes in the natural animal instincts of man take place very slowly—over a long evolutionary period of time—but his outlook, his sense of values change, to some considerable degree, with his environment.

I am afraid most of us in America have had it good, too good, for too long and have gotten soft.

I do not think we, on the average, are as courageous, as ambitious or as moral as our founding fathers. Of course, there are many people today who will dare, will work and have integrity like our forebears. On the average, however, we are, in the words of a very wise friend of mine, "suffering from the ravages of prosperity." We, as a nation, incline to laziness and immorality.

Certainly our environment will continue to change. Certainly our values will change.

There will continue to be conflict between the haves and the have-nots.

There will continue to be a tendency on the part of the older generation to resist change—to maintain the status quo—and a tendency on the part of the younger generation to demand change. The proper route is probably some place between no change and change for the sake of change without due consideration of the effects of change—whether it will improve or impair.

I should like to suggest—well realizing that I am of the older generation and therefore out of touch with the times—that we consider a few values which, to me, are basic. I'd like to recommend that we don't change these until or unless something definitely better has been found or proposed.

They are:
- Courage; physical and moral.
- Integrity; a man's word is his bond.
- Intelligence; a knowledge of things and of people.
- Ambition; a willingness to strive mightily to attain our ends. A determination to progress—but not at the expense of others.

- Patriotism; to put Country above self.
- Humanity; love of people. Living by the Golden Rule.
- Spirituality; a realization that a universe as orderly as it is must be ruled by a Divine Purpose and not by the mind of man.

This seven-point creed by a great American has been the pattern he has set and followed himself. As a man who has been for progress and participated in it, he firmly believes that the values he lists, no matter how "old-fashioned" they may sound, will always be important if the nation is to survive. "I am somewhat distressed to see a few of our young people abandon those values," he said, "without coming up with anything better in their place. I am not against change and I'm not against progress. I am for change as long as it represents progress. Every step that is taken should be a step forward."

Now in his mid-eighties, Doolittle could retire to a life of complete ease and recreation if he so desired. But, a man whose weekly schedules of meetings with aerospace-industry officials, visits to aviation manufacturers, consultations with members of the boards of directors of the several firms he serves, plus hunting and fishing trips would weaken the average person, Jimmy Doolittle has a philosophy about retirement that he expressed to the author:

"I have often pointed out the importance of not taking on too many chores upon retiring. There are so many good things that need doing within the area of one's own cognizance that one is inclined to take on more than he can do well—and there is no satisfaction in a job poorly done.

"The optimum is a good workload where one can continue to serve rather than take from society and still not be under undue pressure so that time will be spared to enjoy some leisure, hobbies and avocations.

"On the other hand, if a well and active person retires to complete inactivity, he is inclined to become a cranky old man—or die of boredom."

Jimmy Doolittle's life has been full of forward steps as he personally pushed back the frontiers of aeronautical knowledge. The nation and the world owe him a great debt of gratitude for the progress he made and caused to be made in the science of aerial transportation.

INDEX

197